PLANNING
YOUR
DISSERTATION

POCKET STUDY SKILLS

Series Editor: **Kate Williams**, *Oxford Brookes University, UK*
Illustrations by Sallie Godwin

For the time-pushed student, the *Pocket Study Skills* pack a lot of advice into a little book. Each guide focuses on a single crucial aspect of study giving you step-by-step guidance, handy tips and clear advice on how to approach the important areas which will continually be at the core of your studies.

Published

POCKET STUDY SKILLS

Kate Williams and Michelle Reid

PLANNING YOUR YOUR DISSERTATION

THIRD EDITION

BLOOMSBURY ACADEMIC
LONDON • NEW YORK • OXFORD • NEW DELHI • SYDNEY

BLOOMSBURY ACADEMIC
Bloomsbury Publishing Plc
50 Bedford Square, London, WC1B 3DP, UK
1385 Broadway, New York, NY 10018, USA
29 Earlsfort Terrace, Dublin 2, Ireland

BLOOMSBURY, BLOOMSBURY ACADEMIC and the Diana logo are trademarks of Bloomsbury Publishing Plc

First published in Great Britain 2013
This edition published 2023

Cover design: eStudio Calamar

Bloomsbury Publishing Plc does not have any control over, or responsibility for, any third-party websites referred to
or in this book. All internet addresses given in this book were correct at the time of going to press. The author and
publisher regret any inconvenience caused if addresses have changed or sites have ceased to exist, but can accept
no responsibility for any such changes.

A catalogue record for this book is available from the British Library.
A catalog record for this book is available from the Library of Congress

ISBN: PB: 978-1-3503-7424-9
          ePDF: 978-1-3503-7425-6
          eBook: 978-1-3503-7426-3

Series: Pocket Study Skills

Typeset by Integra Software Services Pvt. Ltd.
Printed and bound in Great Britain

To find out more about our authors and books visit www.bloomsbury.com and sign up for our newsletters.

Contents

Acknowledgements

Many people have contributed to this guide and we would like to thank them all. First, our thanks to the students who have discussed their dissertations with us over the years. Without the 'works in progress' and outlines of completed studies, this book would not be what it is: a special thank you to the students from Brookes and elsewhere whose work appears here.

Thanks to colleagues at Oxford Brookes University, UK and elsewhere who so generously contributed thoughts for this and earlier editions, from inception to critical review. Thanks also to reviewers who offered generous feedback and advice for this new edition.

Finally, thanks to Sallie Godwin for her inventive and astute illustrations, and to Helen Caunce, Emma Pritchard, Suzannah Burywood and colleagues in the editing and production teams at Bloomsbury who have been endlessly supportive and creative in making this book happen.

Introduction

This book is designed as a guide for students undertaking an extended piece of research at the end of their undergraduate course of study, or as an introduction to independent research for Masters students.

These projects are described in different ways in different institutions, subject disciplines and countries around the world.

What's in a name?

- *dissertation*
- *research project*
- *thesis*
- *extended essay*
- *research paper*

They all require independent research
at the end of a taught programme of study.

In this book, this independent research is most frequently referred to as a *dissertation* (a UK term) or *research project*. Whatever the language, the prospect of setting out on independent research after a taught programme of study can feel like a step into the unknown.

> *How can I possibly write 10,000 words?*

> *This is my opportunity to research something I really want to do ...*

> *I can't imagine working on my own ...*

> *It counts for two credits, so if it's really good I could get a first*

This book is designed as a guide on your research journey. It focuses on looking ahead at each stage so that, by anticipating what comes next, you are better prepared for it.

About this book

Planning Your Dissertation is organised in the order in which you carry out each stage of the work for your dissertation or research project. This is shown as **The journey of your dissertation** on pp. xiv–xv. This, as you will see, is quite different from the order in which you finally present the story of your research in the completed project you hand in.

Part 1 Getting started is about the first steps in planning your research paper or dissertation and introduces some key themes that recur throughout the book.

Part 2 Planning your research ends with an outline of a research plan and proposal, and considers the research and project planning that goes into it.

Part 3 Research proposals and presentations gives practical advice on these two forms of assessment as you move through the milestones of researching, writing and talking about your research.

Part 4 Planning your literature review is about the thinking, searching, reading, (thinking more) and planning that go into a literature review.

Part 5 Thinking about methodology is about the *how* of research, the thinking and planning you need to do to achieve the outcomes you are looking for.

Part 6 What's in a dissertation? This Part is different!

Here in the book you will see outlines of the core structures of dissertations, and some examples of student dissertations from different disciplines illustrating these.

Link directly to our online Dissertations Library! You'll find more outlines of good dissertations. You will see how individual students have adapted the core structures to suit their individual research projects.	
https://bloomsbury.pub/planning-your-dissertation-3e	

Part 7 Writing and argument takes a look at the structures, style and language for writing persuasively.

Part 8 Planning your endgame is about how to showcase your work: how to write a conclusion and introduction and turn your script into a polished finished product.

The journey of your dissertation

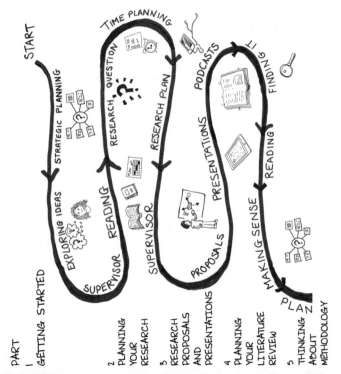

TIMELINE

PART 1
GETTING STARTED

START

STRATEGIC PLANNING

EXPLORING IDEAS

SUPERVISOR

READING

TIME PLANNING

RESEARCH QUESTION

RESEARCH PLAN

SUPERVISOR

PODCASTS

PRESENTATIONS

PROPOSALS

FINDING IT

READING

MAKING SENSE

PLAN

THINKING ABOUT METHODOLOGY

2 PLANNING YOUR RESEARCH

3 RESEARCH PROPOSALS AND PRESENTATIONS

4 PLANNING YOUR LITERATURE REVIEW

5 THINKING ABOUT METHODOLOGY

SUBMIT!

METHODS TO MATCH

USING THEORY

YOUR AIM

CONCLUSION

AIM & OBJECTIVES

ONLINE
DISSERTATION
LIBRARY

PRESENTING RESEARCH

USING 'I'

I think

INTRODUCTION

...NING

LANGUAGE & ARGUMENT

WHAT'S IN A DISSERTATION?

PARAGRAPHS

WRITING PARAGRAPHS

Contents

FIRST IMPRESSIONS

6 WHAT'S
IN A
DISSERTATION?

7 WRITING
AND
ARGUMENT

8 PLANNING
YOUR
ENDGAME

PART
1
GETTING STARTED

Part 1 outlines the first phase of your journey.

- Chapter 1 invites you to stand back and take a strategic overview of what is involved and why you are doing it.
- Chapter 2 takes the first step in becoming a researcher – finding an idea that excites you.
- You are not alone on this journey. You will have a supervisor to advise you. Chapter 3 is about clarifying this relationship so you can make best use of this guidance.

That said, you are embarking on an independent study, and you are both the **researcher** and the **project manager** of this project.

Getting strategic

Why do a dissertation?

The end-of-course dissertation enables you to show that you can do the sort of research you have been learning about throughout your course of study. It will also demonstrate your personal and project management skills, your ability to:

▶ work independently
▶ develop a mature and effective working relationship with your supervisor
▶ manage the project from start to finish – making practical arrangements and meeting deadlines
▶ make an in-depth study of a topic relevant to your future career plans.

Ask strategic questions

The six strategic questions are really helpful in project planning and the answers will help to bring your dissertation into sharp focus.

Used in other books in this series: *Getting Critical*, *Time Management*, *Reflective Writing*.

Read your course materials carefully, and check and recheck regularly online to make sure you have all the information available.

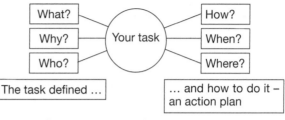

The task defined ...

... and how to do it – an action plan

What exactly do you have to DO? The task defined

Try asking yourself the first three strategic questions, using the prompts below.

What exactly are you being asked to produce?	
How is it described? *Research project? Dissertation? Practical dissertation? Thesis? Research paper? Other?*	
How long/number of words? Are references and the 'preliminary pages' (title page, acknowledgements, abstract, contents, etc.) included in the word count or not?	
What is the guidance about structure, chapters? How many? What goes in them? Approx. length of each?	
Are you given guidance about presentation? Eg font/size, margins, headings, cover sheets?	

Why are you doing a dissertation?	
External reasons: required for an Honours degree, attractive to an employer …	
Internal reasons: a question you want to answer, a need you have identified, personal satisfaction, to excel in your studies …	

Who are you writing for?	
Your primary reader will be a colleague of your supervisor: you have time to get to know what they are looking for.	
Other(s)? Eg work placement mentor. They could be the second reader/examiner in a work-related project. What do they want to see in it?	
Who will help you? What is the role of your supervisor? Who else can help? Librarian, lab technician, contacts?	

As you note down your answers to the first three strategic questions, your project will begin to take shape and become more manageable.

Getting it done – an action plan

Take a few more moments to work through the last three strategic questions – checking through the information you have. The ones below will help you clarify the practicalities.

When are your deadlines?	
When is the deadline for the final submission?	
What are the interim deadlines for each phase/chapter? For registration and other forms to submit? Is there a set schedule or do you have to create your own?	
When are the key meetings and contacts with your supervisor/ course team?	

Where will you do your research?	
Your research and reading? Online? Your uni library? Any other?	
If you plan to do primary research, where will that be? What planning do you need to do for access, permissions, ethical approval? Other practicalities – cost, fares, time, room booking. etc.?	

How will you do it?	
This is what this book is about! And your supervisor will guide you.	

You may be given a clear outline of the stages of your project in lectures, schedules and helpful notes. Equally, you may find you have surprisingly little detailed guidance. If, after you've worked through your course materials and had a go at answering the six strategic questions, you are still not clear, take control and ask.

Pressure to get good grades

Of course you want a good grade!

Successful students focus on their process of learning, overcome their fears, ask questions and proactively seek support on offer from their university (Wong and Chiu 2019).

Who are the people who can help you on your dissertation journey?

Meanwhile, start thinking like a researcher …

Research starts with an idea, a question, an observation – something you'd like to know more about. This is what makes an independent study different. It is your opportunity to research something that interests YOU.

An idea may pop up from anywhere

It could be triggered by …

a news item   an incident at work

a previous course

an experience you've had yourself … or involving family or a friend

a personal interest

something you've read … or observed

something useful to your future career

You may already have an idea for your dissertation. Explore it a bit. First, widen it out – see all the directions it could go in.

Workshop 1: A brainstorm

→ Take a large sheet of paper – A3 is ideal.

→ In the centre draw a circle. In it write your topic with only as much detail as you are confident about right now. If that is quite general, put that down. If you are quite specific in your focus, write that.

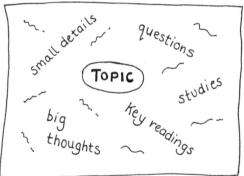

→ Fill the rest of the sheet with everything that pours out of your mind in any order … anything and everything. Don't worry about connecting them – that can follow.

→ Just go for it – take five minutes.

My placement asked me to study one of their services. Something around parents and play.

My dad wasn't allowed to use his medication for diabetes when he went into hospital. Why not?

I'd like to work for a company that takes 'corporate social responsibility' seriously. How do I find out?

I'm a yoga teacher and I know it helps people with back pain. I'd like to find out the scientific evidence ...

It would be good if a new machine for testing samples could be shown to be as reliable as the current slower system ...

I've always loved the outdoors but what opportunities for outdoor play do children get today?

I'd like to work as a wind engineer – I'm doing my dissertation on this.

I come from Greece and study History in the UK. I noticed that Greece features very little on modern European history syllabi, despite the important role it often played.

I'm interested in the links between fitness, heart rate and common health conditions.

I'm puzzled by five Year 3 children who just can't write. Why is this?

I hadn't realised how massive HIV/AIDS is till I went to South Africa. How successful are the various strategies to combat it?

I'm studying tourism but my country is in conflict. What future is there for the tourist industry?

I became genuinely interested in changing lifestyles and the sociology of food and dining out ...

As a student nurse I noticed that many of the residents react very positively to music ...

All these ideas are meaningful. They touch on issues that matter in the real world – a problem to investigate, a question to answer. They emerge at the point where personal interest or experience meets a topic area the student touched on in their course.

Can you add your idea here?

Initial ideas grow and change.
The online Dissertations Library shows outlines of many of the completed dissertations that started with ideas here.

Still stuck?

If your ideas need a bit of coaxing, think methodically about topics and courses you have studied previously.

Workshop 2: Searching for a topic

→ Take a large sheet of paper – A3 is ideal.
→ In the centre draw a circle. In it write 'I'd like to find out more about …'
→ Draw more circles around the big circle, each containing one course or topic area you have previously studied.
→ Take your time …

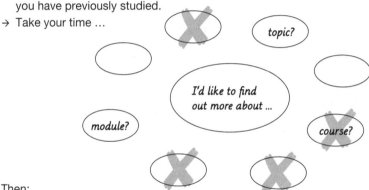

Then:

→ Cross out any you are not particularly interested in.
→ Look at the ones left. Explore these some more.

Where have you got to?

Test out your topic one more time:

▶ Does it interest you?	Why?
▶ Does it matter?	Why?

If you can explain why, you have two key qualities of a researcher:

▶ If it interests you, you will be more able to do the detective work in finding out more about it. Your interest will help you keep motivated in the months ahead …

▶ If what you are researching matters (to you, to your workplace, to others), you will be able to articulate why you are researching it. You have a rationale for your research.

The first sessions are likely to be lectures or group sessions. Do attend these – they lay the ground for your first meeting with your supervisor. Time is precious, and face-to-face time is particularly precious as it is limited. Make good use of it.

Who advises you?

- ▶ *Supervisor*
- ▶ *Teaching assistant*
- ▶ *Lecturer*
- ▶ *Adviser*
- ▶ *Assistant professor*
- ▶ *Faculty*
- ▶ *Staff*
- ▶ *Course team*

Key advisers may have any of these roles.

Meeting your supervisor

Bring to the meeting:

▶ your ideas for what you want to research
▶ any questions or clarifications you want to ask.

Take from the meeting:

▶ your supervisor's feedback on your research topic/question
▶ clarity on how you will work with your supervisor
▶ guidance on your next steps.

Supervisors work in different ways, and while some of the answers to the questions below may be in the guidance, it is a good idea to check them with your supervisor.

Ground rules checklist	Notes
What is the total number of hours your supervisor has to supervise you?	
What does this time allocation include? Face to face or online? 1:1, group tutorials, whole group sessions, email, reading drafts?	
Does your supervisor have a suggested schedule of meetings/contacts and deadlines?	

Ground rules checklist	Notes
How do you contact your supervisor? By email? In what circumstances (if any) is mobile contact acceptable?	
How often are meetings? Are they online or face to face? Do you have to book?	
What if you can't make a meeting? Or need to change one? What notice do you give?	
What preparation do they want you to do before each meeting?	
How will you keep a record of meetings? Notes? Record it? Email a record of key points?	
What kind of feedback will your supervisor give you (written, verbal)? At what points?	
When is your supervisor available and not? Note holiday periods when they are away for some time.	
What should you do next?	

Part 1 has outlined the first steps in your dissertation journey

I
GETTING STARTED

With an idea to take you forward, and a clear idea of the practicalities involved, you can move on with both your research and your project planning.

PLANNING YOUR RESEARCH

Once your supervisor has approved your idea, you can get going on your research.

A research plan (or 'proposal') is a useful milestone and may also be a course requirement. Part 2 is about the thinking, reading and planning that underpins your research plan:

▶ starting the reading to check your idea is researchable and to find your focus or 'angle' (Chapter 4)
▶ developing your initial idea into a working research question (Chapter 5)
▶ time planning for a longer project (Chapter 6).

A practical point

If you plan to carry out any primary research, start making arrangements as soon as possible. Check:

▶ **access** to the setting (people, organisations, locations, equipment)
▶ **processes** such as ethical approval, permissions, requests.

It all takes longer than you think.

---

4 Starting your reading

Read to find out about your topic area – to check that your idea is researchable, to discover what is known out there, to find your focus or 'angle' in a big field. This 'background' or 'preliminary' reading will lay the foundations for your literature review.

The 'literature' is a broad term to cover 'any printed matter' – and of course electronic sources – on which you can draw in your research. Books and chapters are a useful introduction and journal articles are the best source for current research. You may also need to refer to statistics, reports (government, company) and the great wealth of information you can find on the web.

> *Literature:*
> *The body of works that treat of a subject (1860). Any printed matter (1895). Shorter Oxford Dictionary*

Consider things like:

▶ Do you have enough baseline knowledge to make sense of what's out there? If you choose something you are familiar with, you are better able to judge the relevance of material you find.

▶ What themes or topics do you see in the discussions? Choose a topic that relates to issues in your programme of study.

- What concepts or theories are current in your topic area? You will be expected to use these to frame your research.
- What are the debates? You will be expected to show you are familiar with different explanations, perspectives, policies or practices.
- What studies have other people done in related areas? How did they do them?

What kind of sources are you looking for

This (of course) depends on your subject and question. Take a look at past reading lists: websites, books, chapters, journal articles both academic and professional. What type of literature are they? This is a good indication of the type of literature you should be looking for in your research. Think about:

Four types of literature		
1	Theoretical	Presents models and theories for interpreting and explaining patterns in practice.
2	Research	Describes systematic enquiries into policy and practice.
3	Practice	Written by informed professionals who evaluate each other's practice and by practitioners who evaluate their own practice.
4	Policy	Proposes changes in practice that are desired by policy makers.

Source: Wallace and Wray (2021).

Turn your idea into a question ... and see how you can link the elements of your question to 'the literature'.

These examples show this next step for three of the ideas on p9.

Example 1

How does this children's centre help hard-to-reach parents play with their children?	Government and children's centres
	Parents and play
	Play and child development

Example 2

Why don't hospitals allow their patients to manage their diabetes while they are in hospital?	Hospital policies – national and local
	Self-management
	Diabetes

Example 3

Do international hotel chains take corporate social responsibility seriously?	Policies and practices on hotel websites
	Corporate social responsibility
	Strategic management

Your question? + topic links

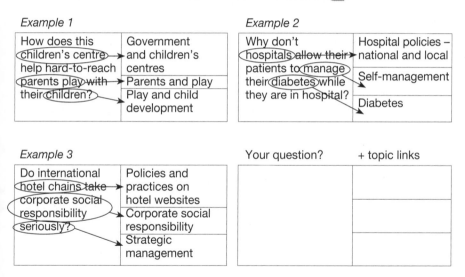

Does this initial reading give you confidence that your question is worthwhile? That it touches on themes rooted in your area of study? That the material is out there and you can find it?

If the answer is 'no', don't give up. It could be that your question is not yet focused enough to be researchable. It might be:

▶ Too topical, too recent for high-quality research to be published yet.
   For example, as we write this (2023), you could not research the long-term impact of Long Covid on a population's health. But you could research the current health effects of Long Covid that we know so far, and compare these to other chronic post-viral conditions to make some possible predictions of long-term impacts.
▶ Too vague, broad and unknowable in its present form.
   You need to work on it, to make it more focused and researchable.

Making it researchable: finding your angle

> Ciara wants to develop a personalised intervention for five Year 3 children (age 7–8) who are not making progress in writing, and to research this for her dissertation.

First, she wants a better understanding of the problem. She looks to the literature:

Why are these five children not making progress with writing?	Child development
	Theories on emergent writers
	Government policies and reviews, National Curriculum

Source: Ciara Fagan (student, Education) with thanks.

But this is all about younger children — nothing to help with my problem of the 7/8-year-olds who aren't making progress with writing.

This is more than a gap. It's a void! Help I'll have to change my topic ...

No, don't change your topic! This is a great topic. It matters, it's meaningful: your findings will make a difference. Stay with it.

Time for reflection ... Am I missing something?

In each case, their English is fluent but, on reflection, not their first language ... Can they write in their first language? Does this matter?

Might it have something to do with cognition?

And more possible avenues for inquiry open up. Research sometimes goes in a straight line, one step after another. More often, you find you have more thinking to do. Just when you think you have nailed it, your research question slips away, and you go back to asking more questions. But it will be the better and richer for it.

Workshop 3: Thinking around your question

When you have done some reading, go back to your original question and try mapping the questions you can now see. You are looking for avenues to go down, possible explanations, lines of inquiry.

→ Take a sheet of paper.
→ Put your topic, problem or question at the bottom.
→ Ask three questions, drawing both on your original thoughts and on new perspectives from your reading.
→ For each, add possible answers, thoughts, further questions.
→ Reflect on the ones you want to follow up.

You are looking for a line of inquiry that really interests or intrigues you – an issue you want to know more about. Start searching, and as you read you may start to see themes and debates about your issue in 'the literature'.

Try rerunning Workshop 3 again, refocusing each time on a new line of inquiry, till you have something you are happy to take forward.

All the thinking you have done so far is the groundwork for articulating your research question in a more precise form.

Workshop 4: <u>What exactly</u> are you <u>trying</u> to <u>find out</u>?

Read this question out loud with the emphasis on the underlined words.

Now answer it as simply and as clearly as you can.
→ Start: '*I'm trying to find out …*' and finish the sentence. No more.
→ Write it down in plain language.

I'm trying to find out …

....

....

You may just have written down your research question. Test it out.

▶ Is it clear to you?
▶ Is it short? A single sentence?
▶ Is it specific? Does it have a single focus?
▶ Does it point you to two or three different areas of literature?

Reconsider your question if:

▶ it has lots of bits to it. Some of these may be sub-questions which you can include as objectives (see pp. 87–8), but take them out of your main research question
▶ it is too broad or general. A more specific question will enable you to achieve more depth
▶ you are not happy with it. You are the best judge of whether your question matches what you really want to know.

PLANNING YOUR DISSERTATION

I'm trying to find out ...

The students above (**Ch 4**) now have a working question to drive their research:

▶ How does a children's centre support hard-to-reach parents in playing with their children?

▶ What prevents patients from managing their diabetes while in hospital?

▶ How do international hotel chains implement Corporate Social Responsibility in their business plans?

The exact wording may change, but the focus is clear.

Do you now have a working question?

Do you now have a working question to drive your research? Write it down.

```
.......................................................................................................................................
.......................................................................................................................................
.......................................................................................................................................
.......................................................................................................................................
.......................................................................................................................................
```

6 Time planning a longer project

A longer project has distinct phases: a beginning, a middle and an end – your deadline. On the one hand, you need to maintain an overview of the whole journey to see what lies ahead and to keep on schedule. On the other, you need to make sure you don't try to micro-plan into the far distant future. You want to see the whole and plan the detail as it comes into focus.

Three stages for planning a longer project

1 **The bigger picture**: deadlines through to hand-in.
2 **The next milestone**: completing a phase/chapter/section/meeting with your supervisor.
3 **The week ahead**: your TO DO list.

Time planning 1: the bigger picture

Plan this quite loosely: the whole journey, and the milestones and deadlines on the way.

Time Management in this series takes a closer look at time-planning strategies.

Workshop 5: The way ahead

Try to visualise your pathway from where you are now (don't look back and include what you've done up to now) to when you hand in your completed dissertation/ project.

→ Take a large sheet of paper – A3 is ideal.
→ Put yourself at the bottom: start.
→ Show your completion point and date at the top: finish.
→ Sketch the journey in between.
→ Mark in the phases of the task.
→ Show the trouble spots and milestones – bits you think you will find tricky, bits you will find stimulating, or straightforward.
→ Mark in the deadlines on the way – set by your supervisor or yourself.

Give yourself 10 minutes.

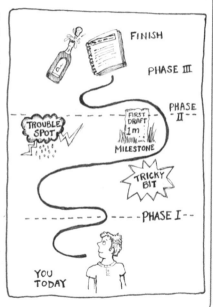

Be realistic! You have other important commitments – other assignments, family, job, sport – a social life, even. Your timeline needs to take these into account.

Now you can plan the phases of your research. What has to be completed before the next phase can start? What do you have to start before your current phase is finished?

Time planning 2: the next milestone

Ideal time plans are ... well ... ideal! In an ideal world you might have started that bit earlier ... but you are where you are. Start from TODAY!

A rough timeline (Workshop 5) may work fine for you. If you are asked to include an *action plan* or *timeline* in a research plan, a Gantt chart gives a neater appearance.

Phase in your research	Month					
	▬					
		▬▬▬▬	■■■■■■■			
		▬▬▬	■ ■ ■			
			▬▬▬▬			
				▬▬▬▬		
					▬▬	

Time planning 3: your TO DO list

There's always something more urgent!

The deadline seems a long way off and other assignments and commitments more urgent, then suddenly the hand-in date is looming!

You do need to micro-plan the week ahead, and what you want to do in each day. This is the point where you have to juggle all the things to do with your life (job, kids, friends, chores) with the small steps towards your project.

Aim to do something towards your research every day – no matter how small. Don't wait for motivation! Put this, along with everything else you have to do, on your TO DO list for

▶ each week
▶ each day.

And tick them off when you've done them. It's a great feeling!

For more on TO DO lists see *Time Management* in this series.

7 Your research plan

Your research plan draws together all the work you have done up to now: your knowledge of the themes of your topic from your reading; the development of your research question. Add to this a plan of action and you will have a useful plan that will help you visualise the phases of the work involved from now to hand-in – and convince your supervisor that you are in control.

There is no set format for a project or research plan. Different institutions, disciplines and departments will vary in the detail of exactly what they require, but there is a common core.

Remember the strategic questions (Ch 1)?

Any research plan needs to offer your reader answers to these key project-planning questions.

Below are points to consider under each question. You may think of others. Check which you will be expected to include and in what order.

Research plan

WHAT?

Your topic
Topic/broad area of interest
Working title, research question, or aim
Specific objectives or sub-questions

WHY?

Think about WHO will be reading this and what they expect to see.

Rationale
Rationale or 'justification' of your question: why are you doing it?
Why does it matter?
Is there a gap you want to fill?
Your personal motivation

A number of HOW? questions

Outline of approach
Reading: Outline of relevant literature
You could be asked to present this as a:
▶ short Context or Background section (referenced)
▶ 'map' of topic areas
▶ list of key sources
▶ annotated bibliography
▶ notes on a small number of key sources

Research design and approach
Here's how I'm going to do it and justification: why *this* way?
Why these theories, frameworks, methods?

Project management

Logistics: the setting/organisation; getting access, contacts, permissions, costs, specialist resources
Documentation: such as ethics and safety forms (if applicable)

Action plan

To show the time you allocate to each phase of your research, interim and final deadlines

A key point about all planning is to ask yourself one last uncomfortable question: *What could go wrong?*

If you can see problematic personal circumstances, plan to bring forward your deadlines.

The unexpected is … well … unexpected.

Build in extra time.

Are you planning to interview people?

Using social media to find the right people may be your first idea. It may also be a good idea – if you do your research carefully.

You can reach out to digital networks or communities of people, such as LinkedIn. You can search for key people in particular sectors, organisations and/or geographical areas. Be aware that people who put themselves out there are self-selecting. They are likely to be:

▶ available to be contacted or interviewed or take part in a survey
▶ willing to engage in discussion and comfortable with putting ideas out there or responding to controversial views.

You would be expected to

▶ respect their anonymity, and not quote them directly (unless they expressly give you permission to do so).

These networks evolve rapidly, and act as 'heat maps' of hot topics, developments and views in a particular area, changing as people join and leave.

Thanks to Professor Gordon Clark, Oxford University, for his advice on digital communities.

8

The supervisor's perspective

For many students, the dissertation or research project marks a transition into the world of work or further study. Some supervisors introduce this external perspective:

▶ *If I was thinking about publishing your project, how would you sell it to me?*
▶ *Time is money. If you multiply the number of hours you spend on your dissertation by the £$ you are paid at work, what do you get? How do you persuade me that your project is worth that?*

This may not be your perspective, and it may not be your supervisor's. Your dissertation will cost you a lot of time and effort and of course you want it to be good: it may also be a shop window for your next step into work or study. Food for thought.

The supervisor perspective

I prefer to think of my role as 'mentor' – more guide than director. It changes the relationship.

Students have been told to make a 30-minute appointment every two weeks. Good students do …

I tell students not to take notes during a supervision and to concentrate on the discussion. Record it – and replay it later.

I expect students to take notes during a supervision, write them up and email them to me afterwards.

If students miss a supervision, it's hard to make it up. The ones who don't attend supervisions or don't submit drafts are the ones who fail.

We expect to see the complete Student Record of Supervision at the last supervision.

The deadlines your supervisor sets are mandatory – non-negotiable.

We set out in writing what students can expect from supervisors and what supervisors can expect of students.

Some students just don't get that this is an independent study – they expect me to give them articles to read and no, I don't write it for them!

Some students don't get it that supervisors have a strict allocation of time and this includes reading and giving feedback on drafts. It's not all face to face …

What's missing from these comments is the warmth, enthusiasm and admiration supervisors often feel about their students and their projects:

> *It's a real joy to see students doing independent work, to see someone branch out, with their own ideas, their own methods.*

(Nick Swarbrick, Lecturer, Education)

Asking for advice on reading – a supervisor's perspective

Which question is more likely to get a positive response?

> *What (books?/ articles?) do you suggest I read?*

Hmm. Unlikely to get a useful response. It doesn't show your supervisor what you've looked at already. It might annoy them as it could look like you're trying to get them to do your research for you.

> *I've found articles about revenue management in large hotel chains, but I've been struggling to find anything for smaller family-owned businesses, could you suggest any sources to look at?*

More likely to get a helpful response. Your supervisor can see the work you've done, the sources you've consulted and the direction you're heading in. They can make specific suggestions.

By this point your research is well under way: you have a working question; a clear direction for your reading; a better understanding of the role of your supervisor – and a project plan to work to. It is time to move on to the next phase of your research.

RESEARCH PROPOSALS AND PRESENTATIONS

The assessment tasks involved in doing a dissertation are milestones that help to give structure and sequence to your research. You will be required to submit a research proposal quite early on in the process. You may also be required to present your research proposal to classmates, face to face or online.

3
RESEARCH
PROPOSALS AND
PRESENTATIONS

SUPERVISOR   RESEARCH PLAN

PROPOSALS   PRESENTATIONS   PODCASTS

Part 3 gives guidance on both the written and oral aspects of presenting the early stages of your research:

▶ your research proposal as an assessed assignment (Chapter 9)
▶ presenting your research to others, in a presentation or podcast (Chapter 10).

9

Research proposal as an assessed assignment

You may be required to do a **research proposal** as a formal, marked assignment as part of your dissertation or research methods module. This provides an interim deadline and an opportunity for early feedback. It also mirrors the process of professional researchers who need to submit proposals for funding and ethical approval.

Check your module handbook for guidance on the content and format of your research proposal. It will usually contain sections similar to the research plan (Chapter 7) and will vary by discipline, department and institution.

Writing a research proposal brings its own challenges:

How do I fit a whole dissertation's worth of reading into a 2,000-word proposal?

Don't worry – you don't have to!

Reviewing the literature

Most research proposals require a short review of the literature of about 800–1,500 words. Your markers know this won't be the same as the full literature review in your final dissertation and don't want you to analyse everything in depth.

This extract from the marking criteria for a proposal shows what is expected:

Draw on academic literature to critically explore the significance of this issue.

Dina is investigating the following question:

Does catering at sports events in the UK mean vegans experience a 'fear of missing out'?

Her research question looks at issues surrounding catering at events: the experience of people choosing veganism, and ideas of exclusion or 'fear of missing out'.

In her research proposal Dina will need to define each of these concepts briefly and introduce the debates surrounding them to show that there is enough literature for her to draw on in her main dissertation. If the gap in the literature is that this experience hasn't been investigated at sports events yet, Dina could draw on literature from other events, such as music festivals, and show that some of it could apply to sports events.

How can I write about research that I haven't done yet?

You're not being asked to!

Justifying the methods

Your markers want to have confidence that your plans are realistic. They also want to see that you understand research methods, and the ways in which different methods affect the type of data you collect.

Here is another extract from the marking criteria for Dina's proposal:

Clearly demonstrate an understanding of the potential impact of research methods and methodologies on the outcomes of your research project.

Again, the markers are not expecting you to have the answers yet, but they want to see that you can select appropriate methods *for your project* (not that you can tell them everything you know about general research methods).

Thinking back to Dina's question above, which of the two extracts below would be more successful in a proposal?

Semi-structured interviews are often used in qualitative research because they are a useful way of gathering individual personal opinions (Bell and Waters 2018). Focus groups also gather qualitative data but in a more social context, and participants can be influenced by the views of others in the group (Bell and Waters 2018).	Fear of missing out can often bring feelings of anxiety and isolation (Larkin and Fink 2016). This is why semi-structured interviews have been chosen for this project instead of focus groups, as they enable people to express their experiences confidentially and individually (Bell and Waters 2018).
Hmm. Sounds like snippets from a research methods textbook ... 😵☹️	*She's using her reading to explain her choice of methods in relation to a specific point in her research ...* 😀

Dina lists the full details of each source in her references section.

An important part of a proposal is being able to use the initial scoping and reading you've done to anticipate likely outcomes and any potential problems.

As part of her exploratory reading, Dina finds that, in the past few years, vegans feel less excluded from music festivals, but the availability of vegan catering can depend on the genre of music and ethos of the festival. She has also read that it can be difficult to get people to open up about feelings of exclusion caused by food, as they fear being labelled as 'picky' or difficult.

Dina can feel confident that what started as a personal interest can become a good, researchable topic. Her proposal will make a convincing argument for the value of her research.

Turnitin anxiety

Can you reuse parts of your research proposal assignment in your final dissertation, or will this be counted as self-plagiarism in Turnitin?

The purpose of a research proposal is to prepare for the dissertation, so some parts of it will be reused. Normally your thinking will move on as you do more research, so the writing in your proposal won't be exactly the same in your final version.

Be honest with yourself; if you are just cutting and pasting large sections from the proposal this obviously isn't good practice. If you decide to include it (probably in a slightly redrafted form) because it genuinely fits, this is fine.

10

Doing a poster, presentation or podcast

You may be asked to present your research as a poster, or in an oral presentation or podcast, as part of your assessed proposal. This is designed to help you to:

▶ anticipate potential outcomes or problems with your research
▶ get feedback early on in the process
▶ gain confidence as a researcher
▶ communicate the value of your research in different forms to different audiences.

Looking into the future, being able to investigate, summarise and present ideas clearly will be good experience – for interviews and future career.

A good place to start planning your presentation is to consider:

▶ Who is my audience(s)?
▶ What is my purpose?

For ideas on how to design and deliver a poster or oral presentation see *Posters and Presentations* in this series.

You may have a number of overlapping audiences, such as your lecturers and also your classmates. You may have multiple purposes, such as convincing people of the value of your proposed research, as well as testing out your ideas and seeking feedback.

Who is my audience?	What is my purpose?
Module lecturer who may also be my marker and/or my supervisor	▶ Convince them that I have a clear, focused and workable project ▶ Show that I have understood and demonstrated the criteria for a good dissertation ▶ Test my ideas and gain immediate feedback
Classmates who may also be asking questions or giving feedback	▶ Test my ideas and gain immediate feedback ▶ Gain a range of different perspectives on my ideas ▶ Interest them in my project and help build connections and community in the class

The instructions for a poster or oral presentation may be left fairly open for you to interpret. Your markers understand that you are in the initial stages of your research, and everyone's dissertation will be very different.

Keep it simple!

Resist the temptation to try and pack all your research for your actual dissertation into your presentation. Stay focused on your **audience** and **purpose** and think of **one** (or at most, two) **clear messages** that you want them to remember at the end.

Your audience usually wants to know **why** your research is needed; **what** you are planning to do; **how** you plan to do it; and **what** you anticipate finding out.

Try using the outlines below as sections in your oral presentation, or as boxes on your poster. But, of course, follow any specific guidance given in your own assignment brief.

Presentation outline

10 minutes with 5 minutes for questions

Sections	Slides	Timing
Outline of the issue	1 slide	2 mins
How my project addresses the issue	2 slides	3 mins
Methods to be used and why	2 slides	3 mins
Anticipated outcomes	1 slide	2 mins
References	1 slide	Not read out – on handout
Questions	Have a slide or two prepared in reserve?	5 mins

Poster outline

Research title / question

Outline of the issue

Methods to be used and why

How my project addresses the issue

Anticipated outcomes

References

It is normal to be nervous when presenting to an audience. Harnessing this sense of anticipation can help to improve your performance

Presenting a proposal brings an added sense of nerves as you haven't done the research yet, so it remains unknown. Here's how you can turn this to your advantage:

Anticipate alternatives: If the next steps of your research are dependent on the results you will find in earlier steps, or if there are a number of possible alternatives, explain this. Show you are aware that outcomes may vary by saying something like:

> *'If I find this result, then I will …' or, 'Of all the possible results, number 1 is the most likely. However, if I find number 2, then …'*

Guide the questions: Let the audience know which areas you would like questions or feedback on. This also helps you to control the topics of the questions. Use phrases like:

> *'I would be very grateful for questions on the research methods …' or, 'I don't have time to explore this further in the presentation, but please ask me about it afterwards …'*

Acknowledge you don't know: It's all right to acknowledge that you don't know something. The opportunity for other perspectives on your plans is exactly what a

---

See *Managing Stress* in this series for more on strategies for managing your reactions to stress.

proposal presentation is for. Don't be defensive about not knowing; instead thank the person and offer to follow up their ideas using phrases like:

> *'That's interesting and I hadn't considered it ...'* or, *'Thank you for the suggestion, I will look into it further ...'*

Creating a podcast

You may have choice in how you present your research. A podcast offers different opportunities and challenges. The challenge is to engage your listener in your project simply by listening to what you have to say – you need to engage them from the first word. The opportunity is to draw out a thread of your research that gives a flavour of your inquiry and leaves them wanting to learn more.

Here's Robert talking about his podcast:

I had to present the idea for my research to my seminar group, and couldn't think how to do it. With one week to go – panic! – inspiration came: do a podcast, tracing the patterns of migration in Brazil through the lens of Brazilian cuisine. I could explore the huge culinary impact/contribution from the African enslaved people, the Japanese influence and the Portuguese too. It had to be in a light, chatty style but have depth and substance. It worked!

Thanks to Robert do Patrocinio for his kind permission to quote his comments.

For an outline of Robert's dissertation see Dissertation 2.d in the online Dissertations Library

Presenting your research is a real opportunity to convey your interest in the topic. Even though your classmates are all working on their own projects, hearing about other people's interests creates a sense of connection. You can ask them more about it, or arrange to study together for support and motivation.

Of course it is also an important milestone in connecting with your supervisor: they will have a good sense of what excites you, where you've got to and what the next steps are.

PLANNING YOUR LITERATURE REVIEW

The literature review is often the first chapter you write. Here you show the knowledge you have gained and the debates you have engaged with. You organise your write-up to lead your reader to your research question and show them the purpose of your research.

4
PLANNING
YOUR
LITERATURE
REVIEW

MAKING SENSE   READING   FINDING IT

This review of the literature may be …	
▶ in a single chapter	See p. 119 and p. 122 and 1.d, 1.i (online)
▶ in two chapters	1.b and 1.c (online)
▶ part of the introduction	See p. 118 and 1.e (online)
▶ not a separate chapter at all, but included as part of the analysis within thematic chapters	See p. 123 and 2.b (online)
For examples, see ▶ in the text and ▶ in the online Dissertations Library	

The steps in organising your research and reading for your literature review are to:

- think about what you're looking for (Chapter 11)
- find it (Chapter 12)
- read it (Chapter 13)
- make sense of it (analyse and synthesise) (Chapter 14)
- and then plan the structure of this section (Chapter 15).

Part 4 outlines these steps. Writing is considered in Part 7.

My supervisor doesn't reply to me!

Check the emails you've sent (are you clear about the advice you need?). Check your supervisor's availability times ... and try asking someone else – seminar leader, a subject librarian, study advice service ...

In going back to the themes you identified in your initial reading, you are in a different place from where you were then. You now know that this is a worthwhile, researchable issue, and you have the tools to get going:

❯ **a working question** to point you to two or three directly related topic areas
❯ **a purpose:** to find the specific strands that will help you answer your research question.

You want to find out …

What is known about your topic areas?	Core knowledge, emerging knowledge, trends
What different approaches and perspectives have other researchers taken?	Concepts, theories and models; studies and case studies
How did they do it?	Could you use or adapt their methods, approach or working tools?

All the time you are asking: how could this help *me* to answer my question?

See also *Where's Your Evidence?* in this series.

Primary or secondary sources?

A **_primary source_** is information collected and written up by the organisation or person who carried out the work at first hand: data collection, a case study, observations, theory, analysis – often published in journal articles.

Secondary sources are written by someone who has read the primary source(s) and summarised or described it in some way – often in a textbook.

Use primary sources wherever you can, and be careful about relying too heavily on secondary sources.

A textbook that summarises a lot of work in the field is a good place to start for an overview. However, you then need to go and find the actual sources so your understanding of the issue is not limited to the short summary in the textbook. You want to get as close as you can to the first-hand experience of the original researcher and use primary sources wherever possible: documents and artefacts, online content, reports, statistics.

In reality, your question will point you to the sources you need, whether it's primary, secondary or somewhere in between. The real question to ask is: _What sources will help me to answer my question?_

See also _Referencing and Understanding Plagiarism_ in this series.

For example

If your question is to find out ...	you might decide to look at
how people's sexual behaviour changed in [response to particular initiatives to combat] the HIV/AIDS epidemic in Uganda (Tom Georgiou, student, Medicine)	▶ specific studies (in peer-reviewed journals) ▶ raw data (held by the Uganda Ministry of Health and international organisations) ▶ systematic reviews (see Ch 19)
whether Corporate Social Responsibility (CSR) is really taken seriously in international hotel chains (Alice Ogle, student, Business and Hospitality)	▶ specific studies (in peer-reviewed journal articles) ▶ online company reports and documentation ▶ trade and special interest publications and websites ▶ theoretical models (books and journal articles)

All are good and appropriate sources for these inquiries.

And what about your question?

You want to find out ...	so you might want to look at
	▶ ? ▶ ? ▶ ?

About 'quality' in sources

If you haven't actually carried out the research yourself, how do you know it's any good? You have two safeguards:

▶ Look for research that has been tested and validated by experts in the field (published in peer-review journals), or research reports produced by reputable bodies such as governments, research institutes, international bodies.
▶ Develop your own critical skills to evaluate anything you think of using. You can try using the six strategic questions (Ch 1).

You're always asking yourself

How convincing is this evidence ...?

Bringing this critical approach to all your reading will help you bring it to your writing.

See also *Getting Critical,* ch. 6 and *Reading and Making Notes,* ch. 14 in this series.

Shelf surfing and Google may have served you well enough in the past. Now, however, you need to develop your research and search skills so that you can use databases effectively to target the quality sources you need.

Searching databases

Computers can't think for you, but they are very good at finding, from a database of zillions of articles, ones that include the keywords you ask them to look for. So think carefully, imaginatively and critically. You are looking for the relatively small number of articles where the keywords come together.

> *Example*
> Research question: *How does political instability impact on tourism planning and development? The case of Zedland.*

For more advice on searching, see *Where's Your Evidence?* in this series.

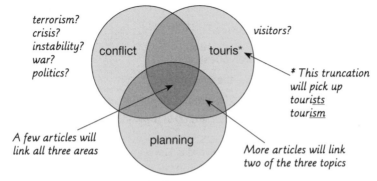

*terrorism?
crisis?
instability?
war?
politics?*

conflict

touris*

visitors?

** This truncation
will pick up
tour<u>ists</u>
tour<u>ism</u>*

*A few articles will
link all three areas*

planning

*More articles will link
two of the three topics*

development?

When you go into the database, you'll see something like this (although you may have to select 'Advanced Search' to get multiple boxes):

Searching: *Selected database*   Choose Databases

	in	Select a Field (optional) ▼	Search
AND ▼	in	Select a Field (optional) ▼	Clear ②
AND ▼	in	Select a Field (optional) ▼	Add row

What will you put in the boxes? Try these strategies.

A search strategy in brief

Step	
1	Write down your research question.
2	Choose your keywords – the main ideas.
3	Think of alternative words for the words you circled.
4	Try truncation (touris*) or wildcard (?) in the middle of the word for alternative spellings.
5	Use AND/OR to combine keywords ('Boolean operators'). OR makes your search broader; AND makes it narrower.
6	*5,742 results?* To limit your results think about: – publication date/year – language – defining your focus or client group more specifically.
7	List the databases you want to use.

Thanks to Hazel Rothera, subject librarian at Oxford Brookes University, for her kind permission to use this material (adapted) and to Emma Coonan for reviewing this section.

As you change and focus your search terms, different articles will come up. Yes, you may feel you are going round and round, but you will be getting closer to what you are looking for.

You get what you ask for!

Without changing your search terms at all, you will get very different results depending on the matching you request: whether you are looking for articles with your keyword(s) somewhere in the *full text*, in the *abstract* or in the *title* itself:

Title: 16 results
Nice and manageable, but are you missing something? You will only find the article if these words are in the title.

Abstract: 253 results
You will see these articles if these words are in the abstract.

Full text: 482 results
You will see these articles if the words are mentioned anywhere in the text! You could drown here ...

Scan your results

A quick search of abstracts produced some likely-looking results. Titles included:

- *Deterrents to tourism in Iran*
- *The influence of terrorism on international tourism activities*
- *From hostile boundaries to tourist attractions*.

Nothing on Zedland, but worth reading the abstracts. Other hits are way off-beam:

- *The myth of wild elephants: a social constructive analysis of elephant–human conflicts ...*
- *The battlefield of the mountain: exploring the conflict of tourism development on the Three Peaks ...*

You just have to get in there, trying different combinations logically and thinking creatively, till you find the articles that look as if they will help you answer your question.

Reading it

> I can't possibly read all that!

No, of course you can't read it all – and you don't need to. Think of yourself as a hook, looking for relevant material to fish out …

Read strategically

The shortest and most useful bit of an article is the **abstract** (100–250 words).

- Have a clear sense of what you are looking for: will this help me answer my research question?
- Get familiar with how abstracts are structured in your discipline.
- Use the abstract to help you decide if you want to read more of the article – or move on to the next.

How to read an abstract

Use the strategic questions as a checklist to help you decide if it's worth reading the full text.

What exactly is it about? What did they find out?

Why was the research carried out? What question does it address? The aim?

How did they do it? Why did they do it this way?

An abstract will usually summarise (in a sentence or two):

1 **Aim** or **research question**: why the research was needed
2 **How** they did it
3 **What** they found/the analysis
4 **Conclusions**: the takeaway points.

Who are the researchers? What are their credentials?

When was it published? And carried out? (often some years earlier)

Where was this research carried out? Where is it published? Is the journal peer reviewed?

Will I read the full article? On the basis of this abstract DECIDE: Do I want to read on? No? No problem! Next ...! Yes? Look at the Introduction of the full text.

And then the big one:
So what?

Why does it matter?

How to read an article

If you decide you want to check an article, you are not obliged to read it all! Read what you need. You can always go back if you need to.

Contents

Abstract

Chapter 1: Introduction

Chapter 2: Literature review

Chapter 3: Methodology

Chapter 4: Findings

Chapter 5: Discussion

Chapter 6: Conclusions and Recommendations

References

Appendices

The intro will show you:
- *the connection between the research and the bigger issues*
- *the writer's argument for the importance of their research*
- *possibly the theoretical approach taken.*

Are you persuaded that it's relevant to you?
No? Then stop.
Yes? What else will you read?

In science, looking at the figures may tell you the main story, and reduce your reading load.

Still curious or undecided?
Read the conclusions (takeaway points) and/or recommendations or implications – the writer's answer to the So what? question.
Decision! Will you read the rest? If you plan to use it, you do need to read it!

Handy tips and pointers!
Even if you don't read it all, glance at these for useful references, or working tools in the Appendices.

This is an efficient way of reading and well worth trying, especially if you consider yourself to be a slow reader. Going in and out of the article several times should speed up your reading. Your understanding gets better as you become more familiar with the topic or line of reasoning – and of course it is your understanding (not your eye movements) that determines the speed at which you read.

Make notes

To help to secure this understanding, **make notes on what you read**: don't rely on your memory. Include:

- the full reference
- brief summary: main points
- evaluation: strengths and limitations
- reflection: how you might use it.

There are other reasons for writing notes as you go. The act of writing helps you to know what you think. Make sure you record the author (full reference) and what they say *separately* to your thoughts and comments. If you do this, you will be able to see who said what in your sources, and be able to reference them. Your reader will also be able to hear your distinct 'voice' as author in your writing, and see how you have used and reflected on the material you have read.

Supervisor's recommendations – too much or too little?
Different supervisors work in different ways. Some give lots of suggestions for reading material and others give very few. Both approaches can be equally frustrating! Remember it is *your* project. Give serious consideration to their recommendations, but the final decisions are down to you!

For more on critical reading and thinking see *Getting Critical; Reading and Making Notes; Referencing and Understanding Plagiarism; Where's your Evidence?* in this series.

Analysis

Analysis is the foundation of critical thinking. This is hard thinking, where you disentangle the strands of thoughts and ideas from your new reading and rearrange them in your own way to make sense of them.

This is a crucial step in being able to use the material you read. If you don't STOP and take stock, you may simply end up describing what this study said, what those researchers did, leaving it to your reader to make the connections with what you're doing. They won't: instead they may say ...

> *Your account is rather descriptive. You need to be more analytical.*

Your reader will want to see what you are **doing** with your reading. The ability to analyse will lead you on to other critical thinking skills ...

The stairway to critical thinking

					Justify
Use critical thinking to develop arguments, draw conclusions, make inferences and identify implications.					
Transfer the understanding you have gained from your critical evaluation and use in response to questions, assignments and projects.				Apply	
Assess the worth of an idea in terms of its relevance to your needs, the evidence on which it is based and how it relates to other pertinent ideas.			Evaluate		
Bring together different sources to serve an argument or idea you are constructing. Make logical connections between the different sources that help you shape and support your ideas.		Synthesise			
	Compare	Explore the similarities and differences between the ideas you are reading about.			
	Analyse	Examine how these key components fit together and relate to each other.			
Start here ☺	Understand	Comprehend the key points, assumptions, arguments and evidence presented.			
Process	Take in the information, i.e. what you have read, heard, seen or done.				

Source: The Open University (2013).

See *Getting Critical* in this series for more on what these terms mean in practice.

Synthesis

Synthesis is when you begin to make sense of the themes that emerge from your reading. The groundwork for this is to arrange your sources and reading into two, three or four main themes.

Workshop 6: Mapping your reading

→ Take a sheet of paper – A3 is ideal.

→ Put your question (as it is now) in the middle.

→ Draw a line out for each of the main themes you have identified (two or three).

→ Use coloured stickies with key points from your reading and stick them near the relevant line.

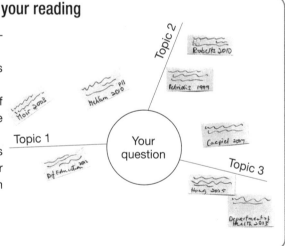

You may prefer to use online tools to help you group and organise ideas, from note-taking apps like Evernote, to software for creating mind maps, like Inspiration or Coggle.

Before paying for any program yourself, check to see if your university provides it for free on campus computers or via a portal like AppsAnywhere.

15 Planning it

You are now well into your literature review. It's time to draw up a plan for writing. See the examples below and Part 6 for decisions students made.

▶ Plan the overall structure: major themes or topics.
▶ Plan the topic areas/sub-themes: work out the order of your topic areas to see the progression of your argument – the flow that will take your reader from the first words you write to your research question.

Example 1: A children's centre

Amina started her lit review with several initial questions:

> Why is play so important for young children?
> Why is play difficult for some parents?
> What can be done to help?

These questions gave her a logical place to start her lit review:

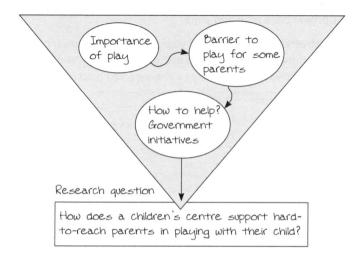

The initial questions firmed up into worthwhile areas to research, drawing in theoretical perspectives as well as policy and practice. This led to the focus and wording of the student's research question.

Amina is now ready to find out for herself what happens in practice and work out the methodology for her primary research.

Example 2: Chronic back pain and yoga

Michaela was interested in the potential of yoga to treat chronic lower back pain (CLBP) and was clear from the start that she wanted to examine the evidence base for this method. In her 'preliminary' literature review she explored both strands of her interest:

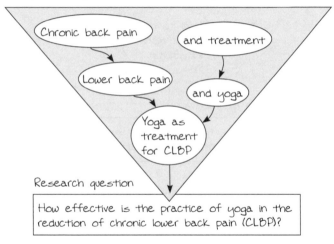

The methodology for this research was the systematic review approach (see Chapter 19).

Example 3: Corporate social responsibility (CSR)

Alice started from a single working question – which proved to have several strands and two phases (explored in two chapters). See how they link.

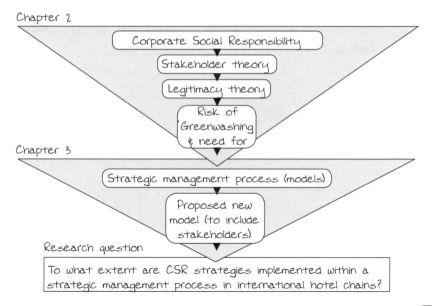

Chapter 2

Corporate Social Responsibility

Stakeholder theory

Legitimacy theory

Risk of Greenwashing & need for

Chapter 3

Strategic management process (models)

Proposed new model (to include stakeholders)

Research question

To what extent are CSR strategies implemented within a strategic management process in international hotel chains?

By linking theories about 'legitimacy' to stakeholder theory, Alice has developed a framework for examining how CSR policies can be implemented through strategic management.

This lays the ground for her examination of the primary evidence of the hotel chains themselves – what do they say they do and how do they do it? – and her methodology for establishing this.

Example 4: Neoliberalism and inequality

Gaia started from a concern about the increasing inequality in India. She wanted to explore the links between this and the economic effects of neoliberalism.

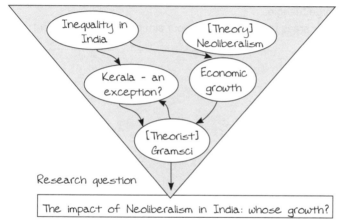

By linking two theoretical analyses, Gaia argues the link between neoliberalism and inequality across India: first, the role of neoliberalism in widening inequality in different aspects of life in India; and second, the theories of Gramsci, in the analysis of an individual state (Kerala).

Workshop 7: Your triangle plan

→ Take a sheet of paper.
→ Draw a large triangle.
→ Map in your areas from broad … to your aim or research question!

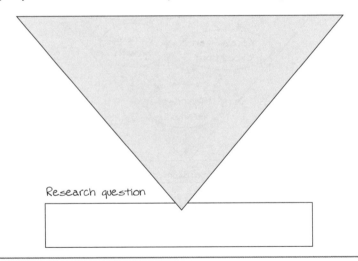

Research question

In your literature review you have shown your reader that you have read, analysed and reflected on the knowledge, interpretations and debates relevant to your research question. You have shown that you are not reinventing the wheel, but 'standing on the shoulders of giants'.

You have made the case for your own research. The answer to your question is not out there in a readily accessible form: there is a gap. You will be providing this answer. The next step is to consider how you will do this.

> Back it up! Email it to someone — or yourself!

When you have completed your literature review, you are ready to plan the 'doing' phase of your research.

5
THINKING
ABOUT
METHODOLOGY

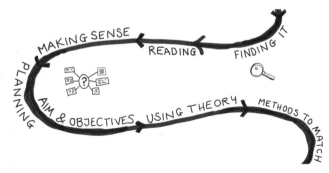

What you actually do in your research will depend on your subject discipline, on what you are trying to find out, and, crucially, the decisions you make about how you will go about finding it out – your methodology. Part 5 outlines some of the thinking you need to do before you set off.

You may decide you want to …

Investigate something yourself and carry out primary research by doing …	
▶ An experiment	See p. 118 and 1.i (online)
▶ Survey and interviews	1.b (online)
▶ Observations	See p. 119
▶ Focus groups, interviews	1.d (online)
▶ Examination/analysis of products, photos, manuscripts, artefacts	1.g and 2.b (online)
Draw together existing theories, models and perspectives in new ways by …	
▶ Critiquing theories and their impact	See p. 122 and p. 123
▶ Reviewing and adapting models and theory	1.c (online)
Create a performance, recording or tangible object and …	
▶ Showing the underpinning theories and approaches	See pp. 126–8

Find the best possible evidence for an intervention or treatment in healthcare by ...	
▶ Using the 'systematic review' approach	1.e (online) and Chapter 19

For examples, see
▶ in the text and
▶ in the online Dissertations Library

What a wonderful world of exploration lies behind these headings! You won't be the first person on the planet to explore your area, so there will be approaches to learn and choose from. But you may well be the first person to research that very specific question and that is truly exciting.

Methodology is all about HOW you do it ...

Your research question has travelled a long way from those initial ideas:

> *My placement asked me to study one of their services. Something around parents and play.*

> *I'd like to find out the scientific evidence ...*

> *I'd like to work for a company that takes 'corporate social responsibility' seriously.*

Your question will now be your guide to how you carry out your research. Do check that the question you started out with still accurately reflects exactly what you want to find out. If your focus has shifted in a major or minor way, rewrite it.

Articulating your aim and objectives

You may be required (or choose) to rephrase your question as an AIM and OBJECTIVES. The aim is your overarching purpose, the whole question. The objectives are the steps you need to take, the sub-questions you need to answer, in order to achieve your aim. Your objectives will correspond to the stages of your research – and you can tick them off as you progress.

For example

> **Aim:** To explore and evaluate the extent to which CSR strategies appear to be implemented within the strategic management process of international hotel chains.
>
> **Objectives are to:**
> ☑ review the literature on [...] defining and analysing [concepts of x and y]
> ☑ evaluate the literature on [z...]
> ☑ develop a framework that will form the basis of [...]
> ☑ analyse and evaluate the application of [...] in [*context*]
> ☑ identify limitations and implications for practice and future research
>
>
>
> Based on Dissertation 1.c in the online Dissertations Library

Workshop 8: Your aim and objectives

→ Take a sheet of paper.
→ Draw an umbrella.
→ Put your research question *as it is now* in it – your overarching question or aim.
→ Start listing the sub-questions or research areas that contribute to the aim (three to five). These are your 'objectives'.

Look again at Alice's objectives (p. 88).

Her first two are to 'review' and 'evaluate' the 'literature' where she will encounter various theories, or ways of seeing, the issues she is studying. In planning to develop a 'framework' she will be using Approach 3 below:

Shaping how you design your research (p. 94)

'Theory' is a slippery term: it encompasses the many ways in which the observations of other people are brought together to help explain and interpret the world around us.

Connecting your own questions with the theories, models and frameworks developed by other people who have puzzled over the same problems is like putting on different pairs of glasses. Each one focuses our attention on a certain set of reasons and interpretations for why things might happen.

One theory doesn't tell the whole story. The fact that any theory only offers a partial view means we can question it, and identify the strengths and weaknesses of this perspective. Different perspectives will lead to different approaches to research.

Identifying a gap in the research for you to fill

All research – and this includes yours – gives some kind of answer to the question the researcher set themselves. The point you want to reach is where you can show that the answer to your question is not out there in a readily accessible form: there is a gap for you to fill.

Chapter 15 shows four students' triangle plans. Each student maps the 'literature' and identifies the theory that will help them answer the question that set them on their research path. Perhaps you did too in Workshop 7?

Look at the five different approaches below. Each shows a different way of using theory to help you answer your question.

Approach 1: Applying a well-established theory to a new or emerging area

Example

> *Applying Diffusion of Innovations theory to understand the early adoption of self-driving cars by the elderly*
>
> In this case, a reasonably well-established theory (Diffusion of Innovations) is being applied to a new or emerging area (the use of self-driving cars by the elderly).
>
> A gap in the research usually isn't entirely novel: it often involves applying existing ideas in a new context, for example:
>
> ▸ Using a different theory to examine an existing issue, *or*
> ▸ Applying well-established theory to a new or different case study, issue or example.

Approach 2: Questioning the theory

Example

How does the concept of 'resilience' affect young adults' mental health?

Here, the theory of 'resilience' itself is being investigated. The fact that the question is being asked in the first place implies that there may be some problems or potential issues with the concept of resilience that need to be examined.

Every theory, by its very nature, provides a limited perspective, so is always open to being interrogated. This could provide the main topic of your research.

Approach 3: Shaping how you design your research

Example

A queer reading of Disney films since 2006

In this example, the student has chosen to examine recent Disney films through the lens of 'queer theory' to focus on the representation of LGBTQ characters and issues.

These issues may not be immediately obvious in the films, so using a theory helps to foreground and justify the direction and the design of the research.

Approach 4: Deciding on the methods you use

Example

The experiences of student nurses studying during the Covid-19 pandemic: A narrative inquiry

In this project, the research methods being used (narrative inquiry) have a particular theoretical approach or philosophy that underpin them and this determines the way the research is conducted.

Narrative inquiry is a form of qualitative research that seeks to understand how people create meaning in their lives as a narrative process. It is often used to highlight the voices and experiences of marginalised groups. As you might expect, in a narrative inquiry, the data gathered tends to be in the form of observations, interviews and stories.

Approach 5: Structuring how you interpret your data

Example

> *Using Social Media Engagement Behaviour (SMEB) to evaluate the effectiveness of social media marketing in encouraging women to check for symptoms of breast cancer*
>
> Here, the student is using a theory (Social Media Engagement Behaviour) as a means of interpreting the data they gather.
>
> The theory gives a framework, or set of criteria, for evaluating how effective the social media marketing has been, otherwise how could we judge what 'effective' means?

Review: How will YOU use theory?

> Look back at your aims and objectives (see Workshop 8)
> ▸ Which of the approaches above come closest to how you might use the theory you have encountered?
> ▸ How might you do it?

The ideas students decide to pursue in their research show that the spirit of inquiry is alive and well! When you are clear about exactly what you are trying to find out, your next question is:

What is the best way to do this?
If you concentrate on this you won't be tempted to rush into the first method that comes to mind …

What kind of information do you need to answer your question?

Look back to the climbing frame sketch on p. 90. A researcher will be asking questions about what they're seeing. For example …

> *How long does each child play on the climbing frame?*

> *What do children feel about climbing on the climbing frame?*

The first question (*How long …?*) looks nice and easy – it will give you numbers, a **quantitative** outcome. But in practice it could be tricky. What counts as 'on' the climbing frame? Sitting underneath it? Running round it? Then there is the *So what?* question: what does the fact of being on the climbing frame for xx minutes tell you about children's views of the experience?

The second question is more obviously tricky: you're looking to elicit accurate responses from young children about 'enjoyment' or 'feelings' – a **qualitative** outcome.

Methods are rarely as simple as they seem! Look to the research methods literature and other studies for ideas and for the debates about the strengths and limitations of the various methods you consider. Make sure you show what you have read (reference it), and explain how it has influenced your decisions about how to carry out your research.

See *Doing Research* in this series for an introduction to research in the social sciences.

What is expected in your discipline?

Look back to any research methods course or other training you have done (eg lab, work or studio) for guidance on questions like these:

What does your discipline place a high value on?	Yes/no How will you do it?
Showing you understand the research traditions ('paradigms') of your subject?	
Showing you understand different theoretical approaches and their implications?	
Justifying your research approach or design	
Detailing your research methods (so someone else could follow what you did step by step)?	
Showing creativity and its theory base?	
Justifying the kind of data you need to answer your question? What information will you gain from counting or measuring – a *quantitative* method? What will you gain from using *qualitative* methods, such as observation, conversation, interviews, analysis of photographs?	
What specific techniques or **specialist materials** or equipment do you need? Can you access them?	

Why do it that way?

In your methodology you need to show that you have a good reason for doing it this way (and not that way). You need to show:

▶ that you have considered the options for the approaches and specific methods you could use (briefly)

▶ why the approach you took and the specific methods you have chosen will give you the sort of information you need to answer your question, *and*

▶ that you can achieve it from a practical point of view (resources and access), and within your timeframe.

When it all goes wrong

Independent research usually doesn't go to plan. A dissertation assesses your research skills and process, NOT whether you get the results you expected.

Make sure your methods match your aims!

All is not lost!!

▶ A questionnaire that only a few people answer is a chance to critique your selection or advertising process.
▶ A failed experiment is an opportunity to show you are now aware of the limitations of your methods.

And finally ... before you meet your supervisor

Do look again at your question (see Workshop 8). If your question has moved or evolved since you last looked at it, make sure your thinking about methodology and the methods you might use has moved with it.

The 'systematic' approach: literature review as methodology

What is a 'systematic' approach?

A review of existing research to answer your specific research question is the methodology now most frequently used in undergraduate and Masters dissertations in healthcare and related subjects.

Students can be confused initially about what this approach involves, especially when it is described as 'literature review as methodology'. Once it can be seen as a methodology in its own right, modelled on the 'systematic review' of evidence for treatments and practices in healthcare, students have a step-by-step path to follow.

Dissertation 1.e in the online Dissertations Library gives an outline of the 'systematic review' approach and shows what goes where.

For detailed advice on literature review as methodology, see Aveyard (2018).

What is a 'systematic review'?

How do you know if one treatment will work better than another, or if it will do more harm than good? (Cochrane Collaboration 2018).

'Systematic reviews' in healthcare and health policy were established by The Cochrane Collaboration to provide answers to this crucial question. Cochrane Reviews are internationally recognised as the highest standard in evidence-based healthcare:

Each systematic review addresses a clearly formulated question; for example:

Can antibiotics help in alleviating the symptoms of a sore throat?

To answer this question, we search for and collate all the existing primary research on a topic that meets certain criteria; we then assess it using stringent guidelines, to establish whether or not there is conclusive evidence about a specific treatment.

(Cochrane Collaboration 2018)

As a student you are not expected to conduct research to these exacting professional standards! But take a look at the Cochrane website to get a feel for the research tradition of the 'systematic review' approach.

You will, however, be expected to develop a clearly focused question to guide your research.

Why use the systematic approach for your methodology?

You need to articulate the reasons why it is the most appropriate methodology for what you want to find out. Perhaps you:

▶ could not generate the data yourself to answer your question
▶ do not want to limit your inquiry to the routine issues you could uncover through your own primary research
▶ want to develop practices based on the best available evidence
▶ have another reason?

The methodology and methods chapter

A 'systematic' approach requires you to be systematic! Keep a notebook or logbook and note down the decisions you make and everything you do at the time (you'll forget very quickly), including things that didn't work out. You will be expected to show each of the steps below in your methodology and methods chapter.

Step 1: How did you develop your research question?

Your decision to develop your research arose from an interest, personal or professional, or both:

> *Why couldn't my dad manage his own diabetes in hospital?*

> *As a student nurse I noticed that many of the residents reacted so positively to music.*

> *I'm a yoga teacher and I just know it helps people with back pain. I'd like to find out the evidence …*

The studies are out there … but you will be drawing together studies that have never been viewed together before to answer YOUR question.

To turn your initial interest into an answerable question, you may be expected to structure it by using a particular framework such as PICO. It will help you dissect your question into its component parts and restructure it to make it easier to find answers.

Formulating an answerable question: PICO (and PICOT)

	The framework	*This means being clear about …*
P	Patient(s)/Population	Profile of patients/subjects you plan to study
I	Intervention/Indicator/Issue	Treatment/intervention given to the subjects
C	Comparison/Control	A similar group of patients/subjects not having the intervention
O	Outcome	How the effectiveness of the intervention is assessed

PICOT: Time may also be relevant to your study

T	Time	In defining the population, eg by age or the timing of the intervention

Example: Laura's PICO analysis and research question

	The framework	*Laura's PICO analysis*
P	Patient(s)/Population	Adults with diabetes in hospital (for unrelated treatment)
I	Intervention/Indicator	Self-management of diabetes
C	Comparison/Control	Self-management of diabetes not encouraged/permitted
O	Outcome	Barriers to self-management of diabetes identified

Her father's experience in hospital started Laura thinking. Using the PICO framework led Laura to the focus and wording of her research question:

What are the barriers to patients managing their diabetes as in-patients?

Step 2: Develop your search strategy

Follow the process outlined in Chapter 12.

Step 3: Work out your inclusion/exclusion criteria and use them

Decide what you really need from the studies to help answer your question. These are your criteria for including – and excluding – studies for your review.

Step 4: Read the abstracts and then the full text of articles on your shortlist

Apply your criteria to each abstract to select articles that meet your criteria for inclusion. Read the full text of those that really look relevant. Exclude those that do not.

Step 5: Other searching: have you missed anything?

Check:

- leading journals in the field for the past year
- websites of key organisations
- full reports where you have found a summary.

In short, use your initiative to find sources that could help you, or satisfy yourself that they are not there.

Step 6: Identify themes

As you read your target articles you will see common themes emerging. Coding papers is a methodical way of doing this – mark each time a particular theme emerges.

Step 7: Decide on your method to critically appraise your papers

In healthcare this is likely to be one or more of the 'tools' in the Critical Appraisal Skills Programme (CASP 2022).

Your supervisor and taught sessions will probably go into more detail on this. Ask if you are unclear.

So, on to your results chapter

Use themes for your analysis: with your chapter organised under themes as headings you will not be tempted to simply retell the 'story' of your articles. You will become analytical as you pull points from several articles to explore the findings on each theme.

For example: Laura identified four themes in her analysis.

1 Hospital systems as a barrier to self-management
2 Staff not handing control of management of diabetes to patients
3 Individual patients' abilities to manage their diabetes
4 Patients' reluctance to manage their diabetes

See Dissertation 1.e in the online Dissertations Library

It's fine to conclude that the evidence is weak: *There is some evidence that … but ….* It shows your integrity as a researcher and that you can see the complexity of knowledge in these fields.

The point about a 'systematic review' is that it is systematic! You have a clear structure and process to work with. You also have the satisfaction of knowing that you are learning to become an effective researcher and practitioner in your field.

The key point to take away from Part 4 is the importance of thinking for yourself HOW you will carry out your research. You gain ideas from the studies you read, you look at how others in your field pursued similar inquiries, you read about the different methodologies used in your field. Finally, you make decisions about how you will carry out your research.

This is what makes this central period of the research project such an enjoyable and satisfying one.

Keep in touch with your supervisor!

Stay in touch by email, online meeting or face-to-face during this time of DOING and WRITING UP your research. Read any feedback you get carefully and reflect on how to use it.

I hadn't seen my supervisor for ages because I was embarrassed about being so behind. I did in the end – so glad I did …

PART
6

WHAT'S IN A DISSERTATION?

> *I can't imagine writing 10,000 words ...*

Sure you can. The 10,000 words will be divided into chapters. Think of these as a series of 1,000–2,000-word assignments. You've done a few of these before ...?!

6
WHAT'S IN A
DISSERTATION?

?
?
?
?

ONLINE
DISSERTATION
LIBRARY
PRESENTING RESEARCH

Part 6 is different from other parts. It shows you two core dissertation structures and offers lots of examples. It is a library of dissertations, some in the book and more online, for you to browse and reflect on.

All the students whose dissertations are outlined received good marks. They all illustrate formats well used in different disciplines. None are 'models' to copy, but they will show you what a completed dissertation looks like in a range of subject areas and the different ways dissertations can be structured.

Here in the book you will find the core structures and some outlines of individual dissertations. We present dissertations with a:

▶ **report-style structure**
▶ **thematic, essay-style structure**
▶ and a **balance of written and practical work**.

20 Dissertations Library

> **Our online Dissertations Library** offers a wider range of outlines for you to consider, grouped under the **report-style** and **essay-style** headings.
>
> **Take a look** and pick up a few ideas to take you forward …

https://bloomsbury.pub/planning-your-dissertation-3e

Have a good browse!

Our Dissertations Library, on the page and online, shows outline Contents pages of student dissertations – you may find this helpful in planning your chapters and sections. If you have the opportunity to look at complete past dissertations in your subject area and from your institution, do take it! (Check they are good ones!)

Look at:

▶ **preliminary pages**: title page, official paperwork, abstract, acknowledgements
▶ **contents:** chapter structure and titles; subheadings and numbering
▶ **chapters:** what goes where; relative length of each chapter
▶ **introduction** and **conclusion,** and the link between them
▶ **use of illustrations**
▶ **appendices** and **references**.

and overall:

▶ evidence of coherence, progression and argument
▶ writing style.

We hope the examples in Part 6 will help you work out for yourself the structure that best suits your inquiry.

What's in a title?

While you are browsing, note the style and wording of the titles. It may help you decide on the final wording of your title. Titles can take various forms:

Title form	Example
Question	*What are the barriers to patients managing their diabetes as in-patients?* (Dissertation 1.e online)
Statement	*The political ecology of HIV/AIDS in the Eastern Cape, South Africa* (Dissertation 1.d online)
Catchy bit + statement of what you researched	*Measuring counts? The role of design in maintaining healthy behaviours* (Dissertation 1.g online)
Statement + catchy question	*The impact of neoliberalism in India: whose growth?* (see p. 122)
Examples from ▶ dissertations in the text and ▶ online Dissertations Library	

A basic report-style structure

Report-style structures follow the basic outline of a scientific academic paper. They tend to suit research in which you are making hypotheses, gathering and analysing your own data, or following a specific methodological approach (such as a systematic literature review).

They are often seen in subjects such as science, technology, psychology, some business dissertations and the social sciences.

Contents

Abstract

1   Introduction

2   Literature review

3   Methods

4   Results

5   Discussion

6   Conclusion

References

Appendices

Report-style structure example 1: Biomedical Science

Title: Evaluation of an automated urine analyser for use as a negative screen on urine samples

Abstract
The current situation: the problem
The investigation: what was done and how
What was found
Conclusion and recommendations

1. Introduction and Literature review:
   1.1 The urinary tract
   1.2 Incidence and infection
   1.3 Pathogens and pathogenesis
   1.4 Treatment
   1.5 Laboratory diagnosis
   1.6 Aims of the project

2. Materials and Methods
   2.1 Materials
   2.2 Methods

3. Results
   3.1 Machine's performance at predicting urinary tract infection
   3.2 Determining of optimum cut-off values for screening

4. Discussion
   4.1 Study population: unintended bias in data group
   4.2 The machine tested: strengths and limitations
   4.3 Potential of machine – cautiously positive
   4.4 Interpretation of results linked to previous findings in the literature
   4.5 Future investigation and suggested improvements

5. Conclusion
Positive indications ... but larger study needed for more accurate assessment

Reference list

Appendices
The documentation of the research:
   1. Safety (COSHH)
   2. Risk assessment
   3. Detailed results (raw data)

Thanks to Laura Dunn (student, Biomedical Sciences) and to the John Radcliffe Hospital, Oxford, for their kind permission to include this reference to her work.

Report-style structure example 2: Education

Title: Ways to play: how does a children's centre support hard-to-reach parents in playing with their child?

Abstract
Context of workplace and issue
Aim
How the study was done
What was found
Conclusions and implications for workplace practice

1. Introduction
1.1 Why this topic?
  - Personal interest / opportunity
1.2 Outline of workplace priorities
  - The need for better understanding of specific issue
1.3 Research question and objectives
1.4 Overview of chapters

2. Literature Review
Overview of chapter
2.1 The problem as identified in the literature
2.2 Area 1 [the importance of play]
2.3 Area 2 [the importance of adults / parents in encouraging play]
2.4 Area 3 [why do some parents have difficulty with encouraging play?]
2.5 Conclusion

3. Methodology
Overview of chapter
3.1 Research approach
3.2 Selection of methods
3.3 Data collection (including ethics)
3.4 Data analysis
3.5 Validity and reliability

4. Results and discussion
Overview of chapter
4.1 Communication between centre staff and parents
4.2 Modelling and demonstrating forms of play
4.3 Toy and book lending
4.4 Child-parent events

5. Conclusions
5.1 What was learnt?
5.2 Recommendations and implications for practice

References

Appendices
1. Letter of invitation
2. Interview outline
3. Transcripts
4. Details of observations
5. Ethical consent / approval

Thanks to Amina (student, Education).

As you can see from the examples:

▶ The **literature review** may be part of a longer **introduction** chapter.
▶ The **research questions, aims and objectives,** or **hypotheses** may come at the end of the literature review.
▶ The **methods chapter** may be divided up into specific sub-sections, for example: participants, materials, procedure.
▶ The **results** may be combined with the discussion into a single chapter.
▶ The **conclusion** may also include **recommendations.**

A basic essay-style structure

Essay-style structures are more thematic and tend to suit research that analyses texts or theories in detail. They are often seen in subjects within the humanities, such as history, film studies and politics, as well as some theoretical business dissertations.

Contents

Abstract

1 Introduction

2 Theme 1

3 Theme 2

4 Theme 3

5 Conclusion

References

Appendices

Essay-style structure example 1: Politics and international relations

Title: The impact of neoliberalism in India: whose growth?

Abstract
Aim
Research questions
Theoretical approaches
Argument
Conclusions

1. Introduction
1.1 Focus of study
1.2 Key concepts [neoliberalism and inequality]
1.3 Research question 1
1.4 Key theorist [Gramsci]
1.5 Research question 2
1.6 Outline of argument and chapters

2. Literature review
2.1 Overview
2.2 Role of theory
2.3 Outline and critique of theory [neoliberalism]
2.4 Outline and critique of theorist [Gramsci]
2.5 Conclusion

3. Historical Overview
3.1 Pre-liberalisation policies
3.2 1966 Liberalisation attempt
3.3 Economic reforms during 1980s
3.4 Crisis leading to reforms
3.5 Liberalisation of 1991

4. The effects of neoliberalism
4.1 Impact on class
4.2 Impact on rural poor
4.3 Impact on employment
4.4 Impact on production

5. Study of the state of Kerala
5.1 Gramscian analysis

6. Conclusion
6.1 Restatement of argument
6.2 Summary by chapter
6.3 Implications for development

References

Thanks to Gaia Pagliara for her kind permission to refer to her Masters dissertation.

Essay-style structure example 2: Business – hospitality

Title: Dining out for distinction

Abstract
Aim, context and broad approach
Key theories and relation to topic (dining out practices)
Location of specific focus (dining out) to broader social change

Chapter 1. Introduction
1.1 Introduction to topic area
1.2 Rationale
1.3 Research aim and objectives
1.4 Methodology / approach
1.5 Chapter structure

Chapter 2: The Sociological constructs of taste
2.1 Introduction
2.2 Tastes of necessity and tastes of luxury
2.3 Social class and the body
2.4 The role of the domestic meal
2.5 Summary

Thanks to Jessica Barwell (Business and Hospitality student) for her kind permission to refer to her work.

Chapter 3: Postmodern food behaviours
3.1 Introduction
3.2 Individualisation
3.3 Communification
3.4 Stylisation
3.5 Informalisation
3.6 Summary

Chapter 4: Contemporary dining out cultures
4.1 Introduction
4.2 Democratisation of luxury
4.3 The commodification of experiences: Dining Out
4.4 Cultural omnivorousness and hierarchies of knowledge
4.5 The existing lower class
4.6 Summary

Chapter 5: Conclusion
5.1 Conclusion
5.2 Limitations
5.3 Recommendations and future research

References

As you can see from the examples:

▶ An essay-style dissertation may have a **separate literature review chapter**.
▶ Or an essay-style dissertation may have a **longer introduction** that includes a **review of the literature and methodology**.
▶ **Thematic chapters** start with a **brief introduction** and end with their own **conclusion**, similar to an essay.
▶ There can be as many **thematic chapters** as needed.

In creative and practical subjects such as architecture / art / dance / design / product design / fashion / film / media / music you may be offered a choice in the balance between the practical and written components that together make up your dissertation.

In these styles of dissertation you will be **making** or **producing** something (a product, performance, demonstration, artefact, design or presentation) and also writing a **theoretical discussion** or **rationale** explaining what you produced.

Once your research is under way, ask yourself
▶ **How** am I going to present my research findings?
▶ And **why** is this the best way?

In consultation with your supervisor, you will have to decide on the balance between theory and practice that best suits you and how you want to communicate your research process and outcomes. Bring your ideas to your supervisor – their support and advice will be crucial throughout your dissertation period.

Your decision about this relative weighting needs to be made early on as it will influence both your research process and your production. In all models, the practical work will be expected to illustrate, test or explore the thinking in the written research.

Your options may look something like this:

Weighting		Balance between components
Written	Practical	
100%	0%	100% weighting on the written component is similar to previous outlines. It may include case studies, critical analyses of design strategies, performances, illustrations, or annotations and commentary.
75%	25%	Significant weighting to the written component requires a substantial critical/analytical commentary showing the relationship between practice, theory and thinking.
50%	50%	Equal weighting to the practical and written components requires a careful division of time, and a balance of creativity and research between the two parts.
25%	75%	Greater weighting to the practical component allows more time to develop a performance, website, lecture-recital, event, structure, display, installation, portfolio. Thoughtful, concise explanation of theoretical influences, rationale and design process is essential.
0%	100%	Usually an exceptional option only if agreed with your supervisor early on. Likely to include a 'viva' or interview in which you explain your process, thinking and research methods.

Do the sums – the word count of the written component should reflect the percentage weighting it carries. Knowing what you are aiming for will help you see the shape of the project ahead and where to concentrate your energies.

Example of different practical and written weightings (Dance)

The diagram below shows three options for structuring your dissertation: 100% written (in the middle) and two 50/50 options.

50/50 Single idea	100% written	50/50 Lecture-demonstration
... explored through	Introduction	... of a specific section or theme
Writing Choreography	Chapter 1 Chapter 2 Chapter 3 Conclusion	Combining – spoken word – visual performance

Be prepared to explain your decisions and to discuss them with your supervisor.

Many thanks to Dr Clare Parfitt, Reader in Popular Dance, University of Chichester, UK, for her valuable advice underpinning this section, and for her kind permission to adapt images from her course materials.

In the 50/50 single idea option, the written analysis and choreography sit side-by-side as two separate, but closely linked, components, each providing explanation for the other. The main themes and ideas run throughout both components.

In the 50/50 lecture-demonstration, the 'lec-dem' is a presentation of the themes in one section of the project (in this case, Chapter 2 of the dissertation). The spoken and visual performance in the 'lec-dem' is weighted equally to the theoretical aspects developed in the written analysis in the other chapters.

The 100% written option is a dissertation containing thematic chapters using an essay-style structure.

What will be in your dissertation?

In Part 6 you have seen some of the many ways of organising your inquiry and structuring your dissertation or research project. These completed dissertations are polished products, each one the outcome of drafting, redrafting, getting it wrong, getting it right, reflecting the decisions the writer made at every turn.

It's your turn now to work out how your dissertation will be. One thing you can be sure – there is no one-size-fits-all magic formula. Your dissertation will reflect your own inquiry and be shaped by your own hard work and the decisions you make along the way.

You've reached another milestone – one you may be asked to share with other students, classmates or in a student conference. The advice on presenting in Part 3 still holds good. By now, however, you will have a clear sense of the focus and findings of your research to present to your audience.

Some departments require students to give a presentation (sometimes called a 'defence' or 'viva') as well as submitting the written dissertation. Researchers often have to present their work at various stages during their project, and communicating the outcomes of the research near the end of the project is a useful way of consolidating and synthesising it.

The principles of good presentations for research proposals (See Ch 10) apply equally to presentations near the end of your project:

▶ Consider your audience and purpose.
▶ Keep it simple.
▶ Have one clear message to communicate.

The main difference is that the focus is more on the final few chapters of your dissertation and explaining what you found, what you learned and what this means.

Be selective with your findings: By now you will probably have a lot of data, so resist the temptation to include it all in your presentation. Instead, go back to your research questions (plus any aims and objectives) and select the findings that help you answer your main questions.

▶ If you include any graphs or tables on your slides, explain the main overall patterns or trends on the graphs, so you don't leave the audience guessing, or overwhelmed with data.

Acknowledge the limitations: An important part of the research process is learning from the experience and being able to see how any limitations in your research design may have affected the results.

▶ Don't try to gloss over, or hide, any limitations, even if everything went wrong! (see pp. 52–3). Being able to talk honestly about limitations will increase your authority, not diminish it!

So what? Apply your results: The main purpose of a research presentation is communicating the contribution to knowledge that you have made. What do we know now that we didn't know before? How will your conclusions help improve practice in your area, or what recommendations would you make based on them?

▶ Leave your audience in no doubt about the value and application of your research.

It may seem harsh to make you do a presentation on top of writing a long assignment, but the process of preparing for the presentation and getting your findings and conclusions clear in your mind should make the final writing stages easier.

PART

7

WRITING AND ARGUMENT

In writing your dissertation, you are not simply writing about something, but taking your reader with you on your journey of discovery – through your argument.

Part 7 focuses on writing: it shows how to ensure your writing is well-structured, persuasive and that your 'voice' comes through in an appropriate way.

7
WRITING AND
ARGUMENT

Paragraphs are important: here's why

Paragraphs have a *structure*

▶ A paragraph develops **one main idea**.

▶ This main idea is usually expressed clearly in one sentence – the first, or **topic,** sentence.

▶ Paragraphs have a beginning, a middle and an end. The sentences in the middle explain, develop, evidence or modify the main idea in the topic sentence. The last sentence often returns to the idea in the topic sentence to show how it has developed.

Many of the approaches here have developed from previous publications. See *Getting Critical,* in this series.

Paragraph structure has a *purpose*

It makes it easier to:

▶ **Read**: the main idea is first, and you know that this idea will be developed before you move on.

▶ **Plan**: each paragraph develops a single point. You can plan by mapping out the points.

▶ **Write**: new point, new paragraph. Start each paragraph with a clear statement of the point you are making, then add detail.

How to write a paragraph

To write a paragraph, start with an idea of what you want to say, a point you want to put across. Through the paragraph develop this idea into a short block of text, and your section builds up – paragraph by paragraph.

A paragraph plan

1 **Start with the topic sentence** to express the main idea.
2 **Explain or define any abstract, key or problematic terms** to clarify the topic sentence.
3 **Show your evidence** to support your main idea or argument in the topic sentence.
4 **Comment on the evidence** to show how it supports or develops the main idea. If appropriate, mention other evidence (examples, studies, experiments, interpretations) to widen the discussion.
5 **Conclude.** Look back to your topic sentence and ask yourself:
   ▶ How have I moved on/developed the main idea in it?
   ▶ Where am I going next?
   ▶ Then write the last sentence.

This basic structure can also be used for more sophisticated writing.

Workshop 9: Paragraph planning

Below is a paragraph from the literature review of a Masters dissertation. How does it match the paragraph plan? Try adding the numbers of the paragraph plan to the text.

In politically unstable countries the roles of stakeholders may be different to those in developed or developing countries (Petridis 2013; Mansfeld and Hong 2020). Stakeholders are also likely to have a different profile and priorities to those in more stable countries. In less stable countries the private sector is likely to play a key role in pressurising the government to allocate time and money for tourism development. However, as Mehlim (2019) points out, the government may regard tourism planning as a low priority in the context of the political situation in the country. He acknowledges that while not-for-profit organisations and other professionals may play an important role in other respects, the government may not be responsive to their efforts in relation to tourism planning. In these circumstances, Czepiel (2018) argues that the private sector can become the driver in tourism planning in politically unstable countries. It can draw together the different groups to form a persuasive group of stakeholders, prepared to seize the opportunity to position past or even current conflicts as tourist attractions.

Kiran (student, Business and Tourism).

Turn the following page upside down to see how the paragraph has been planned:

In politically unstable countries the roles of stakeholders may be different to those in developed or developing countries (Petridis 2013; Mansfield and Hong 2020).[1] Stakeholders are also likely to have a different profile and priorities to those in more stable countries.[2] In less stable countries the private sector is likely to play a key role in pressurising the government to allocate time and money for tourism development.[3] However, as Mehlim (2019) points out, the government may regard tourism planning as a low priority in the context of the political situation in the country. He acknowledges that while not-for-profit organisations and other professionals may play an important role in other respects, the government may not be responsive to their efforts in relation to tourism planning. In these circumstances, Czepiel (2018) argues that the private sector can become the driver in tourism planning in politically unstable countries.[3/4] It can draw together the different groups to form a persuasive group of stakeholders, prepared to seize the opportunity to position past or even current conflicts as tourist attractions.[4/5]

1 Topic sentence

2 Explain/define

3 Move to supporting evidence

3/4 Supporting evidence, discussion and argument intertwined showing the position of the writer

4/5 Comment conclusion and look ahead to next paragraph

This paragraph is persuasive – and draws the reader to the writer's bold concluding point. By the time you reach the end, you realise that this is where the writer was going to from the first sentence. You have been carried there through a subtle blend of argument and evidence. How does it work?

A paragraph is, in effect, a unit of argument. Each paragraph builds on the one that went before, and leads to the one that comes after. In this way you develop a persuasive argument in a logical and coherent way.

This chapter takes a closer look at how the writer of the paragraph above progresses their argument through choice of language – at how the 'moves' of a paragraph are intertwined with the sources the writer draws on.

The writer does not comment directly on the sources they use. Nevertheless, the point they make and the direction of their argument are perfectly clear to the reader: the writer has a clear 'voice'. This invisible current is what is meant by having a 'position' or line of reasoning. You are providing the 'golden thread' to take the reader from where they are when they start reading your work, through to where you want them to be – on your terrain.

Let's take a closer look at how it works:

> *Argument:*
> *A connected series of statements intended to establish (or subvert) a position; a process of reasoning.*
> *Shorter Oxford Dictionary*

For more on 'voice' see *Where's Your Argument?* in this series.

Tracing the 'golden thread of argument'

In politically unstable countries the roles of stakeholders may be different from those in developed or developing countries (Petridis 2013; Mansfeld and Hong 2020).[1]	**1 Topic sentence** Sets out the argument – and engages the reader: *how will this writer progress this idea of the 'different' role of stakeholders in these countries?*
Stakeholders are also likely to have a different profile and priorities to those in more stable countries.[2]	**2 Explain/define** The reader wants to see the writer is in control and can propose a sensible focus for the analysis and argument to follow: *differences narrowed to 'role' and 'priorities'.*
In less stable countries the private sector is likely to play a key role in pressurising the government to allocate time and money for tourism development.[3] However, as Mehlim (2019) points out, the government may regard tourism planning as a low priority in the context of the …	**3** Move to **supporting evidence** Careful steer by the writer to focus the reader on the key point of the discussion: *how to draw the government into supporting tourism.* The argument is set up.

political situation in the country. He acknowledges that while not-for-profit organisations and other professionals may play an important role in other respects, the government may not be responsive to their efforts in relation to tourism planning. In these circumstances, Czepiel (2018) argues that the private sector can become the driver in tourism planning in politically unstable countries.^{3/4}	**3/4 Evidence** and **argument** intertwined – showing the writer's awareness of the debates in the field and the **position** in relation to them. *Comment is implicit through the choice and sequence of studies referred to. Note the impact of the verbs: points out/ acknowledges/argues.* *A new voice – by referring to Czepiel at this point, the writer takes the next step in his argument as the lead-in to his conclusion.*
It can draw together the different groups to form a persuasive group of stakeholders, prepared to seize the opportunity to position past or even current conflicts as tourist attractions.^{4/5}	**4/5 Comment, conclusion** and **look ahead** to next paragraph. Returning to the argument of the topic sentence: *the word 'persuasive' to describe the stakeholders shows the writer's position, drawing the reader onto the writer's ground.*

The conclusion shows the distance the writer has travelled from the topic sentence, and as readers we have followed his line of reasoning. We are ready now for the next paragraph, where he has the opportunity to convince us – or not – of the validity of his proposition.

Words that help argument

You saw from the paragraph above how carefully the writer picks his way through the research. The language he uses helps to position himself in relation to the writers whose work he draws on:

> *As Mehlim (2019) points out …*
> *Czepiel (2018) argues …*

And where the writer had no need or wish to go into the detail of a source in a general point, he tells the reader where to go for the evidence: … *(Petridis 2013; Mansfeld and Hong 2020).*

Careful choice of verbs shows your voice. You can signal doubt ('claims'), caution ('suggests'), specific interest ('points out') and so on. This is a fundamental skill in conveying your argument and will lift your writing from being merely 'descriptive' to being analytical and evaluative.

See how it's done:

Six magic verbs		
Smith (2020)	*points out* *argues* *maintains* *claims* *concludes* *suggests*	... that preventative medicine is far more cost effective, and therefore better adapted to the developing world.

Source: Based on the University of Manchester's *Academic Phrasebank* (2023).

Using these words effectively gives your reader a clear insight into what you think about what you read – and this of course is what your dissertation supervisor wants to see. It works something like this. As they read, the tutor will be thinking ...

What does this tell me about what my student thinks about ...?

The student writes	The tutor thinks ...
Smith (2020) ...	
points out that ...	*Ah! This student has picked out something interesting ... they have read thoughtfully.*
argues that ...	*They've done some sustained reading and can follow Smith's line of reasoning ...*
maintains that ...	*I feel a 'but' coming ... This student is keeping a bit of distance here. Interesting research but ...?*
claims that ...	*My student is being careful here. Either it's emerging research, or they aren't convinced by it.*
concludes that ...	*My student is picking the key point of the research, a useful takeaway point ...*
suggests that ...	*A mature and balanced way of presenting a perspective ...*

Six magic words? Yes, they are, and there are plenty more words like these to choose from. They lift your writing and open up a conversation with your reader. And that is exactly what you want to achieve.

Writing isn't a cruise around the islands!

This is a cop-out by the tour guide! You want more than a patchwork of snippets from other tour guides.

Your reader wants more too: from introduction to conclusion, via lit review, methodology and discussion, your reader is looking for the 'value-added' from you. When you are positioning yourself in relation to the different authors you have read, your reader wants to hear your voice:

Where are YOU in all this? The So what? What next? questions

▶ *Well, is it the biggest? And why are you telling me?*
▶ *So what if it's volcanic? What difference does that make?*
▶ *Why this boring quote about tourists?*

This is the 'descriptive' writing tutors really don't want … and we hope that now you can see why!

Four words to ruin your writing

~~Said …~~   ~~States …~~   ~~Highlights …~~   ~~Looks at …~~

All this tells me as a reader is that you have read the source (probably) but you have absolutely nothing to say about it!

'States' does have one important use: to report on a key point from an authoritative source (eg government policy or report, industry standards, professional practice guidelines) before you move on to discuss it. For example:

Ofsted (2022 p16) **states** that ninety-seven per cent of all early years providers were judged either good or outstanding at their most recent inspection. However, Hartman (2022) **points out** that …

You report directly and neutrally …

… before commenting on different views, and showing your own position through how you refer to your sources

Source: Ofsted (2022). *Annual Report 2020/21: Education, children's services and skills.*

How visible do you want to be in your writing?

This depends on the research traditions of your subject area and what you decide or are expected to do. In some subjects (science subjects for example) the focus is on the process, not on the researcher/writer, so the writing style avoids 'I'. In others (some social sciences and humanities) the researcher is more visible as part of the process, and the selective use of 'I' is appropriate.

Check with your supervisor early on. Does your supervisor agree with the points below? Always follow their advice!

Reflections
If you are asked to include reflections (for example, on what prompted your interest in your research area, or how you would use your findings in your practice), use 'I':

See *Reflective Writing* in this series for advice on writing style.

- *My interest in the subject arose when ...*
- *I was offered the opportunity to ...*
- *By doing this study I can say now that my practice is supported by evidence ...*

Introducing and concluding chapters

It is good practice to introduce and conclude each chapter (briefly) to signpost your reader through your work. Decide on the style for this:

Visible author: using 'I'	Less visible author style
In this chapter I explain the process I followed ...	*This section of the study will examine ...*

Or you can move between both styles:

Visible author: using 'I'	Less visible author style
I draw on the theoretical approaches of ...	*Chapter 2 reviews the literature on ...*
I draw on primary qualitative data ... then put forward the case for ...	*This section presents the aim and objectives of ... It then puts forward ...*

In your methodology

This is where you set out what you did: you have to make judgements about how visible you are in your account, especially in primary research.

Visible author: using 'I'	Less visible author style
All the papers I identified were ...	*Subjects were asked to ...*
By situating myself within the treatment community I was in a position to ...	*The survey was developed by using ...*
I felt it was not appropriate to conduct research in this way ...	*The questionnaire was devised with the help of ...*

Difficulties arise when students try to record their actions in detail, or are asked to include reflections but *not* to use 'I'. This can produce clunky and awkward writing:

> **Try not to write like this!**
> *... the restricted timeframe forced the author to ...*
> *The research process gave the researcher invaluable experience in ...*
> *The author completed an electronic database search ...*

Part 7 has outlined some core writing skills and decisions you will draw on as you write up your research. These are not decisions you make once: like everything else in research, it is an iterative process – you go backwards and forwards – and though it may not always seem like it, you do move on.

Keeping going …

To get going, take 15 minutes to
- ▶ review what you did yesterday
- ▶ adjust a diagram
- ▶ sort some references
- ▶ sketch out something new.

If you get stuck, take a break!
- ▶ Do something active
- ▶ Go outside
- ▶ Boil the kettle …

When you go back to it with your brain refreshed, something may just click.

Part 8 is about the endgame. With all your major chapters drafted, they now need to be transformed into a polished and persuasive document.

As **researcher**, your job is pretty much done. As **writer**, you still have work to do: writing your conclusion, introduction and abstract. As **project manager** and **editor**, you take control, bringing all the strands of your dissertation together to that wonderful moment when you submit the final version.

Submit your final version via the Turnitin dropbox by 16:00 on Friday Week 8

Time planning!
Skim through Part 8 quickly and write down how long you think you need to allow to hand-in.

....

Be clear about what you are aiming for

Remind yourself what a good completed dissertation looks like. Part 6 gives you a flavour, but the real thing is better.

Your assessors will approach your dissertation rather like you look at others. You are in a hurry and anything unclear will annoy you. You use the structure to guide you: a dissertation has a beginning, middle and end. So does each chapter, section and paragraph. You want to see something like this:

Dissertation	Chapter	Section	Paragraph
1 **Introduction**	**Chapter 2: xxxx** Introduction – this chapter /...	**2.2 xxxxx xx xxxx** Introduction/link	The five times more to attract new customers that it does to keep an existing customer happy. Conversely it needs to be considered that even within a customer base not all patrons will be profitable to the company. In retail banking for example, the This definition covers the important point that the needs and objectives of both the customer and the organisation must be satisfied. Satisfying customers should be an essential part of marketing activity for it is cheaper to satisfy and thereby retain existing customers than it is to obtain new ones (Oliver 2015). According to Masterson et al (2016) it costs approximately five times more to attract new customers that it does to keep an existing customer happy. Conversely it needs to be considered that even within a customer base not all patrons will be profitable to the company. In retail banking for example, the existing customer happy. Conversely it needs to be considered that even within a customer base not all patrons will be profitable to the company.
2	2.1		
	2.2		
3			
4			
5	2.3		
6 **Conclusion**	**Conclusion**	**Conclusion**/link	

Structure helps the reader locate whatever they are reading within the whole: the writer promises at the beginning, and delivers at the end. It makes for a happy reader!

What are the examiners looking for?

Check your guidance and make sure you understand what it means: ask if in doubt. Whether set out formally or not, assessors will be looking for evidence of what you have learnt (learning outcomes) and will be assessing your work against assessment criteria – something like this:

Overall, your readers will be looking for

Strong internal consistency, making the research project a convincing whole, clearly addressing the research question in:

▶ argument
▶ logical structure
▶ use of evidence (primary/secondary) to support argument
▶ critical and reflective awareness of strengths and limitations
▶ clear conclusions and recommendations.

Specifically, this will show in your

- *Research question*: problem or investigation: clear aim, objectives, focus, convincing rationale
- *Literature review*: range of reading; grasp of theoretical principles and applications; relevance to research question; independent research; depth of knowledge and understanding
- *Research methods*: appreciation of methodological issues; rationale for approach chosen; systematic information/data gathering and analysis; critical awareness of strengths and limitations
- *Findings*: presentation of data and analysis; identification of themes
- *Synthesis*: bringing together research to show you've grasped the relationship between them
- *Presentation*: consistent structure; no errors or typos; appropriate writing style (including integration of citations); correct referencing.

With thanks to Cathy Burgess, Faculty of Business (Oxford Brookes University), for her kind permission to include the above. Adapted and with additions from Science, Education and Health and Social Care.

The key point is that the dissertation should be a *convincing whole* with a logic and argument that runs from start to finish.

Drafting and redrafting 1: your main chapters

You've been focusing on getting the ideas and information down. Now look at the whole and be prepared to rearrange and prune.	**Edit it** for the big picture: • Check content, structure, balance. • Introduce and conclude each chapter/section to show your argument. • Leave enough word count for your introduction and conclusion chapters.

> Take special care to back up while you are editing and cutting and pasting between versions.

These two chapters are key in crafting your dissertation – and in the impression you make on your reader.

▶ The introduction is written or revised *last*, when you know exactly what you are introducing.
▶ Write the conclusion after all the other chapters – *before* you write the introduction.

In this way, you know that your promise of what lies ahead (in the introduction) is indeed fulfilled (in the conclusion). Equally, you can be sure that the point you arrived at in your conclusion is indeed a logical progression from the introduction.

Writing your conclusion

In the conclusion you **look back** at the whole dissertation journey and set out the takeaway points. You also **look forward** to show why your findings matter, how your research relates to the issues you identified in choosing your topic and in working out your research question. You suggest how your findings might be used or implemented in, for example, your workplace or industry.

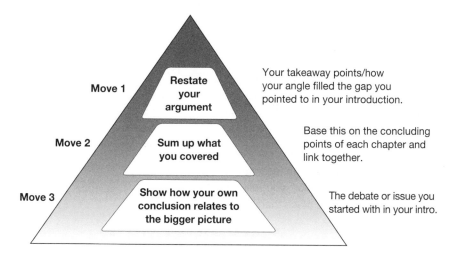

Move 1 — Restate your argument — Your takeaway points/how your angle filled the gap you pointed to in your introduction.

Move 2 — Sum up what you covered — Base this on the concluding points of each chapter and link together.

Move 3 — Show how your own conclusion relates to the bigger picture — The debate or issue you started with in your intro.

Your reader will look at your conclusions before they read the whole. Do articulate clearly what you have achieved and learnt. It will motivate your reader to trace the process through your dissertation.

The conclusion

▶ is usually a short, free-standing chapter at the
  end of your dissertation;
▶ includes a summary of your key points;
▶ contains no new material. If you think of a
  last-minute addition, place it in the relevant
  chapter or leave it out.

In the table (below) are elements of a conclusion
which may be used as subheadings or in
combinations. Consider which you will include
and the order in which you place them.

Take a look at the dissertations in Part 6 and in the online Dissertations
Library – look for dissertations in a field similar to yours.

What's in your conclusion?	Yes? No?
Restatement of aim, or **problem** you addressed	
What you learnt: key findings	
Limitations of your research What you didn't do, couldn't do; the limits of your data, methods or circumstances	
Implications for – practice – policy – personal learning	
Areas for further research – where your research might go next – unanswered questions/future research	
Recommendations If appropriate (see for example p. 119 and p. 123)	
Reflections on personal learning If explicitly required. Write in a 'reflective' style, using 'I'	

Writing your introduction

This section is about that part of the introductory chapter where you:

▶ introduce your reader to your topic
▶ interest them in what you have to say – your argument
▶ lead them to your aims.

By the end, you want your reader to be saying, *'Yeah! Go for it! I quite see why you want to research this, and I really want to see what you find ...'*

Write your introduction straight after you've written your conclusion, setting aside any earlier versions. This is how you make sure that your conclusion and introduction are joined at the hip!

Think of your introduction as a series of moves:

Move 1 **The context/background/bigger picture**
Introduce your reader to your topic/issue/problem

Move 2 **Your research area**
and why it matters

Move 3 **Specific research areas**

Move 4 **The gap** in previous
research and rationale
for your research

Move 5 **Aim** or
**research
question**

Overview of chapters
Use this to show progression and linking, so it's more than just
Ch. 2 does this, Ch. 3 does that. This is your reader's road map.

The conclusion and introduction

Using the 'moves'

The topic sentence of each paragraph indicates the content of the paragraph – and shows the moves. In this introduction, some moves include several paragraphs.

The effects of listening to music on people with dementia	Moves
Dementia is a broad term … It is claimed that nearly all people with dementia will develop some significant behavioural problems …	Move 1
…	
Agitated and aggressive behaviours are frequently thought of as … The use of medication to manage …	Move 2
…	
Non-pharmacological techniques … The soothing effects of music …	Move 3
…	
However, the quality of some of the research […] has been questioned …	Move 4
leading to …	
Why my research is needed to fill the gap! And the aim of my research …	Move 5

Vidya (Adult nursing)

Workshop 10: Your introduction in five moves

→ Draw yourself a large inverted triangle (as on p. 163).
→ Number the moves from 1 to 5.
→ Write a single topic sentence for each move. You may decide to start with Move 5, the aim.
→ Read the five sentences out loud to yourself.

You can then develop each move into a couple of sentences – and see the shape of your introduction emerging.

Your introductory chapter may also include additional elements. These include:	
▶ methodology	See p. 123 and 1.c, 2.b (online)
▶ literature review leading to aims, especially in science subjects	See p. 118
▶ hypothesis (linked to aims)	
▶ preliminary literature review	1.e (online)
▶ your personal or practice reasons for choosing this topic to research	See p. 119 and 1.e (online)
▶ scope and limitations	1.b (online)
For examples, see ▶ in the text and ▶ in the online Dissertations Library	

Drafting and redrafting 2: add conclusion and introduction

Make sure you promise (in the introduction) what you deliver (in the conclusion) and that they reflect any shift in focus that happened along the way.

Edit it to make sure the points come across clearly: flow, linking, logic, topic sentences, references, word count.

Check the appearance of your pages: indentations, spaces between paragraphs and sections.

Look at your pages upside down – you will see the visual impact without the distraction of reading it.

Can you see the golden thread of argument running from start to finish?

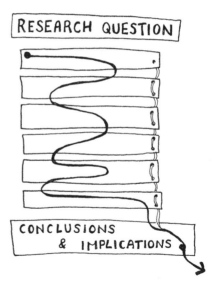

Become an editor!

Finally! Take off your writing hat and become an editor. Leave at least a day since when you last looked at it so you come at it cold and see what's really there (not what you *think* is there).

Be organised about version control. Date the footer and file name of each version, and back it up!

Drafting and redrafting 3: is looking good	
Add Contents, Lists of Tables, Figures, Acknowledgements, Abstract, Appendices. Then sit down for a good (but critical) read …	**Proofread** for anything that doesn't make sense or sound right; write short sentences. Check for spelling, punctuation, grammar, part sentences, typos, lookalike words popped in by the computer, anything with a wiggly line.

Watch out for:

▶ Too many or too long quotes: shorten them to 'keywords', or summarise (keeping the reference).
▶ Funny-sounding phrases where you cut and pasted.
▶ Tenses, especially bits from earlier drafts of your methodology. This is now 'what you DID' (past tense), not what you planned to do (future).
▶ Check your references. Every source in the text should be listed in the references and every listing should be there in the text. Follow the recommended style meticulously.
▶ Anything that especially annoys your supervisor (check previously marked work).
▶ Your favourite errors!

Does it make sense?

If it doesn't make sense to you, it won't make sense to anyone else! Try reading it out loud, or ask a friend or family member to read it.

First impressions and last thoughts

When you click 'submit' to send your final dissertation, all your hard work will be waiting in that file. Your supervisor – supporter, mentor, guide – will open it as an assessor and examiner, ready to scroll down and read. What will they see?

Title page

Check you meet the formal requirements of your title page, and any additional required wording or pages, such as statement of originality.

Acknowledgements

Thank everyone who helped or supported you, with an indication of how they helped:

▶ your supervisor by name (a MUST!)
▶ anyone else who inspired you in some way
▶ participants/subjects
▶ people who offered practical help
▶ friends and family.

But maintain confidentiality/anonymity here too!

> *And my thanks to Mrs Pugwash, headteacher of Pudsey School, and Class 2 teacher Mrs Flitworth, and those lovely children, Mehmet, Emmie, Caz, Rodrigo, Leon, Annie ... WHOOPS!!*

Abstract

You've read a lot of these, remember? Check the abstracts of dissertations you have access to, and abstracts in journal articles in your subject area.

An abstract consists of four short statements (often run together) summarising your research.

1 **Aim** or **research question**: why the research was needed.
2 **How** you did it.
3 **What** you found/what your research shows or suggests.
4 **Conclusions**: the takeaway points. Recommendations if appropriate.

Keep it clear and short. But do work on it – it is your shop window.

Contents

Your reader will want to get an overview of the structure, organisation and coherence of your dissertation.

Bald chapter headings are not enough:

Chapter 1: Introduction
Chapter 2: Literature review
Chapter 3: Methodology
Chapter 4: …

But don't drown them in detail:

> **2. Literature review**
>
> 2.1 xxxxxxxx
>   2.1.1 xxxx xxxxxxx
>   2.1.1.1 xxxxx
>   2.1.1.2 xxxxxx
>   2.1.1.3 xxxxxxxx
>   2.1.2 xxxxxx xxxxxxxxx

Give enough detail to show the relationship between topics in the chapter:

> **Chapter 2: Greenwashing? The role of stakeholders and concept of legitimacy**
>
> 2.1 Overview of chapter
> 2.2 Stakeholders and CSR
> 2.3 The role of legitimacy and CSR
> 2.4 Greenwashing
> 2.5 Conclusion

Lists of tables, figures, illustrations

These give an indication of the detail of your work and the thoroughness of your research.

And at the end …

References

These come immediately at the end of your text.

In humanities the 'Bibliography' is usually placed last, after any Appendices and Acknowledgements.

Appendices (where used)

These are not a dumping ground for anything you can't fit into your word count! They are material your reader may wish to refer to in order to see the sources for the points you discuss in your text.

See also *Referencing and Understanding Plagiarism* in this series.

For example, in your text:

... a list of questions was developed from noting gaps in the literature (see Appendix 2) ...
... the University Code of Practice (see Appendix 4) was ...

Appendices might include:

▶ raw data or summary tables of primary research results
▶ data collection tools used: eg questionnaire, prompt questions for interviews, interview transcript, photos, observation records, record sheets
▶ analytical tools: eg CASP (in Health and Social Care), measurement tools, statistical tests
▶ procedural records: ethical approval letters of permission, participant information sheet, consent form, safety considerations.

You are now very close to THAT moment when you submit all your hard work ...

Time planning, again!

Do you need to revise how long you need to allow for the final stages?

Then there is the unexpected – which, by definition is …
err … unexpected!

The hand-in moment is the destination of a long journey with many phases. Celebrate your achievement, sleep it off and enjoy the warm glow of achievement.

This long project at the end of your course of study is a major achievement. It will play a part in determining your overall grade: you have demonstrated your ability to become expert in a specific aspect of your studies.

You have demonstrated your personal, research and project management skills to:

✓ set up your own inquiry
✓ work independently
✓ carry out research – and become expert!
✓ develop a mature and effective working relationship with your supervisor
✓ manage the project from start to finish.

Presenting for real

By communicating your research at various stages during your project, you will have developed valuable communication skills and topics to talk about at interviews or in new roles.

> *Tell me about a time when you demonstrated problem-solving skills …*

> *Ah … I can talk about the time when the lab technician threw out all my soil samples, but I managed to reconstruct a useable data-set from already published results …*

It will stand you in good stead in your next steps whatever they may be.
Good luck – and enjoy!

References

Aveyard H (2018). *Doing a Literature Review in Health and Social Care: a Practical Guide*. 4th edn. Maidenhead: Open University Press.

Cochrane Collaboration (2018). *What is Cochrane evidence and how can it help you?* Available at www.cochrane.org/what-is-cochrane-evidence (Accessed 31 July 2022).

Critical Appraisal Skills Programme (2022). Available at www.casp-uk.net/ (Accessed 31 July 2022).

Open University (2013). *Critical Thinking*. Open University Press.

University of Manchester (2023). *Academic Phrasebank*. Available at www.phrasebank.manchester.ac.uk (Accessed 7 October 2022).

Wallace M and Wray A (2021). *Critical Reading and Writing for Postgraduates*. 4th edn. London: SAGE.

Wong B and Chiu Y-L T (2019). 'Swallow your pride and fear: the educational strategies of high-achieving non-traditional university students'. *British Journal of Sociology of Education*. 40(7) pp. 868–82.

References to other books in the Pocket Study Skills series

Bethell E and Milsom C (2014). *Posters and Presentations*. London: Bloomsbury.

Coonan E (2020). *Where's Your Evidence?* London: Bloomsbury.

Cooper H and Shoolbred M (2016). *Where's Your Argument?* London: Bloomsbury.

Cooper H and Shoolbred M (2019). *Using Feedback to Boost Your Grades*. London: Bloomsbury.

Godfrey J (2023). *Reading and Making Notes*. 3rd edn. London: Bloomsbury.

Joseph K and Irons C (2018). *Managing Stress*. London: Bloomsbury.

Thomas G (2017). *Doing Research*. 2nd edn. London: Bloomsbury.

Williams K (2022). *Getting Critical*. 3rd edn. London: Bloomsbury.

Williams K and Davies M (2017). *Referencing and Understanding Plagiarism*. 2nd edn. London: Bloomsbury.

Williams K and Reid M (2011). *Time Management*. London: Bloomsbury.

Williams K, Woolliams M and Spiro J (2020). *Reflective Writing*. 2nd edn. London: Bloomsbury.

Useful resources

Pears R and Shields G (2021). *Cite Them Right.* 12th edn. London: Bloomsbury.

This much-expanded edition gives models for references for the most used referencing styles. Watch out for the most recent edition. *Cite them right online* is available via many university libraries.

RMIT *Learning Lab*. https://emedia.rmit.edu.au/learninglab/

From the home page, choose your area: writing skills, study skills, assessment tasks, postgraduate and more. Excellent advice is linked to the writing skills you need – all readily accessible.

University of Leeds (2023). *Dissertation examples.* https://library.leeds.ac.uk/dissertation-examples

More example dissertations! A library of good-quality dissertations from a range of undergraduate and taught Masters courses – be aware that they all come from the University of Leeds, so they may follow some conventions specific to this university.

University of Manchester (2023). *Academic phrasebank*. www.phrasebank.manchester.ac.uk/

This superb resource is for anyone looking for words and phrases to use in their writing, especially if you find yourself using only two or three verbs to introduce a source. It is user-friendly and well organised – a must!

University of Sheffield (2023). *Academic literacy resources.* www.sheffield.ac.uk/eltc/language-support/academic-literacy-resources

If you would like to improve your academic English, this comprehensive and clear resource provides step-by-step instruction on all aspects of academic literacy, including examples and self-assessment quizzes to support you.

Index